The Delicate Art of Whale Watching

Joana McIntyre Varawa

Updated and with a new Foreword

Sierra Club Books

San Francisco

The Sierra Club, founded in 1892 by John Muir, has devoted itself to the study and protection of the earth's scenic and ecological resources—mountains, wetlands, woodlands, wild shores and rivers, deserts and plains. The publishing program of the Sierra Club offers books to the public as a nonprofit educational service in the hope that they may enlarge the public's understanding of the Club's basic concerns. The point of view expressed in each book, however, does not necessarily represent that of the Club. The Sierra Club has some sixty chapters coast to coast, in Canada, Hawaii, and Alaska. For information about how you may participate in its programs to preserve wilderness and the quality of life, please address inquiries to Sierra Club, 730 Polk Street, San Francisco, CA 94109.

Copyright © 1982, 1991 by Joana McIntyre Varawa
All rights reserved under International and Pan-American Copyright Conventions. No part of this book may be reproduced in any form or by any electronic or mechanical means, including information storage and retrieval systems, without permission in writing from the publisher.

Sierra Club Books paperback edition: 1991

Library of Congress Cataloging-in-Publication Data
Varawa, Joana McIntyre.
    The delicate art of whale watching / Joan McIntyre. — Updated and with a new foreword.
        p.   cm.
    ISBN 0-87156-550-1
    1. Cetacea—Hawaii—Lanai.   2. Whale watching—Hawaii—Lanai.
I. Title.
QL737.C4V37   1991   90-48285
599.5—dc20   CIP

Cover design by Bonnie Smetts
Map by Ronna Nelson

Printed in the United States of America on acid-free recycled paper.
10 9 8 7 6 5 4 3 2 1

FOREWORD TO THE NEW EDITION

When this book was written I had had the profound luxury of being able to camp for two years on a cliff overlooking
Manele Harbor on the Hawaiian island of Lana'i. Lana'i at
that time was, metaphorically if not actually, the western fron-
tier of the United States. A tiny red dirt island dreaming in
the sun. Commercially it had been developed as a pineapple
plantation and thousands of acres of pineapple carpeted the
uplands in spikey regimented rows. Lana'i City, more like a
village than a city, was tucked beneath a forested ridge and
was the only place of habitation. Clustered in the city were a
few hundred wooden cottages that were home to a population
of about 2,000 people, whose primary occupation was pineapple. The rest of the island was wild land.

A history of land acquisition and consolidation over the
past 100 years had brought the entire island under single own-
ership except for a few remnant acres of native-owned land,
and because it was almost entirely privately owned and un-
fenced the island was totally accessible. We all camped and

fished and hunted and wandered the many jeep roads that led to miles of pure coastline. It was a local life-style, and an easy one.

The island was important to me for it gave me the time and the place to see and to think, to relax, to perceive that what the whales and dolphins could offer was vastly different than our expectations. And so I conceived of writing this "guide" to watching whales.

Now the island is undergoing massive change and is being developed as a world-class tourist resort. Many of the places I described will not be found as I described them—and whale watching, once a simple pleasure, is now a multi-million dollar business.

... And so it seems relevant to bring this book back as a gentle recollection, not only of Lana'i, but of a simpler time. I do not fear for the whales and dolphins, but I care for them, and I would trust that you care for them as well. They were here hundreds—perhaps thousands—of years before we came. Hopefully they will still be here long after we are gone. Caring for them can be our legacy to the seas that brought us forth, and that still wash these incredible shores.

Joana McIntyre Varawa
Lana'i, 1991

An Introduction

FOR THE LAST FIVE YEARS or so I have lived on or near the edge of the sea, watching, from a distance, the whales and people come and go, meeting briefly in or on the blue water. I came to the sea with great expectations. I was an expert already, a writer filled with words, and a city person filled with ideas. My profession, so to speak, had been the politics of whale saving, and that profession had wearied me and turned me into a bitter person filled with doubt and anger.

So I went to the sea to find out for myself what all that was really about—to wash out of me the anger and the weariness. I had seen my own best intentions turn into stupidity and the best intentions of others turn into righteousness. It was time to return to the great mother of us all, not with a project or a program, but with a barely spoken prayer that she cleanse me of my confusion. I called it re-search, which to me meant to look again for the source of the knowledge, the knowledge that had been obliterated by too many ideas, too much reading and talking, and not enough listening and silence.

I went to the sea, to the edge of silence, to the great natural rhythms of night and day—the surf, the stars, the passage of the moon to tell my time—and I waited for my mind to quiet and for new experience to come to me and to heal me.

This little book is written out of that experience and out of my belief that we choose what will inform and nourish us. The ocean with the creatures that live in her is a great physician of the body and of the soul.

In Hawai'i there is an expression, *mālama 'āina,* which means "care for the land," for the land is food, and place and medicine and all things that nourish. There might equally be a saying *mālama kai* that means "care for the sea," for she is the mother and giver of life and strength and wisdom.

This little book, then, is not a field guide in any conventional sense. Its aim is not to help you with keys and tables to be able to identify species and subspecies of whales and dolphins by name or to assure you that they will indeed be found here at this place, now, at this time, for such assurances are only good on paper and have little to do with real time and tide, which are the determinants of experience. And as for instant naming, I have been taught what that is worth by watching visitors ask local people the names of the fish they are catching, and, when told, still know nothing, not even to understand or pronounce the names given, for naming without knowing is one of our easiest habits and one that teaches us the least. It is almost as if the name itself, like a card pasted over the thing named, hides it from view and makes us each more full of nothing.

So do not expect much in the way of convention here, for my desire is to paint instead a few little pictures of the sea: the coast, the land, the time of year, the hint or promise of something there, seen briefly, and if not attended to, not seen at all. We are all searching for something, and often when we find it, we are too busy to notice.

For many of you, to go out and seek whales and dolphins is a planned adventure. You have your tickets in hand, so to speak. For others, it may be a chance desire. It is a fine bright day, and the sky is beckoning. The shops no longer give you

pleasure, and so here you are—in one paradise or another
—with nothing to do. The nicely painted sign above the handsome boat invites you to go "whale watching," for this or that
amount, and so you pack what you believe is appropriate gear
and set out, hopeful that you will see whales.

However you reach the pier, at one time or another you
cross the slight boundary between land and sea and set foot on
some boat or another to go out on the water and watch for
whales and dolphins. With you may be friends or strangers, a
chance assemblage, or even a group led by an expert or guide.
But with whomever you go, we all are novices or beginners,
for even the most expert know nothing but their own ideas.
And each man's or woman's ideas are equal in nature, where
human thought is always trying to net reality, and yet the net
catches nothing but more thought and ideas, for who can
catch a sunrise or the shape of a curling wave?

This guide will caution you about carrying too much bag-
gage, for we all burden ourselves with extra things that we
think we might need, but then our time becomes one of caring
for our luggage—while the moon sails serenely free above us
and the whales sing freely beneath us. We fuss with tape recorders and cameras, trying again to net the image, which,
when returned from the processors, can be held in the hand
—as if the moon could be held, or the whale's voice carried in
a suitcase.

So this is to advise you to go light and free, with as little as
you can manage, with as open a mind and heart as you can
carry. That is my own advice to myself, and I promise not to
tell you anything which I do not accept as my own best
counsel.

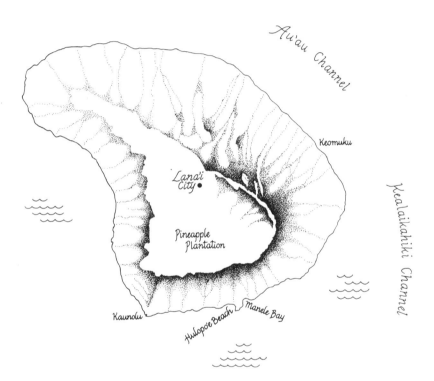

Au'au Channel

Keomuku

Lana'i
City •

Kealaikahiki Channel

Pineapple
Plantation

Kaunolu

Hulopo'e Beach   Manele Bay

The Coast

The coast is a beginning place, an edge. In the high icy northland, where whales sing to the accompaniment of glaciers roaring into the sea, or in the tropics, damp and misty in the green humid light of a rainy morning, the coast is where we meet —whales and people, sea and land. The rain-laden sea wind meeting the high mountains or the soft rain settling like mist over the sand. Open any book and you may find a map that tells you nothing of a particular morning or even how sharp the rocks, but that calls a name to you, which you follow to reach the place where you are a stranger. Then comes the need to put foot on ground, to look around.

A visitor on the beach once asked me where was the shade. I looked at the trees, the patches of shade, the birds fluttering in the lacy branches, the far-off mountain, and I realized that the lady was lost—for the shade was all around her and could be found by looking. Another time, while I was walking in the fields—the whole island opened like a great vessel around me: the mountains clear, clouds sailing overhead, the sun glittering on the distant sea; even the main road to town was clearly visible—some other visitors came riding up in a jeep, raising a great cloud of dust, and pointing to the map in hand, asked me to tell them where they were. I opened my arms and said, "Here, this is where you are."

Then walking on the high ridge of Haleakala, looking across the channel at the immense volcanoes, seeing a whole island sunning itself—the bays, the white-edged coast. I look at the clouds rushing in the high trade winds, the swell of the sea as she wraps around the point and, bathing in the fresh pure water that issues from the earth, transparent and icy, I hear a short squawk from a small black box tell me of the weather.

A map can offer a name, but each place named has qualities that can only be found by being there. Each coast is itself and has many moods, and yet is enduring, for the rocks move very slowly; and the human eye is too tightly focused to notice small things, like a flicker of white in the water or a flash of green in the shallows.

Look then, through your eyes, not your mind, letting them go a little misty so you can see movement, letting them go soft so that color is clear.

Watching for whales is much like watching for a lover. There is much expectation, and there is much time spent where there are no whales to see. Then what is there to do in the hot sun staring at the sea?

I have always seen whales when I was not looking for them, but was looking out, my eyes open for an instant and not staring at some words in my mind. But I spend much time staring at the words in my mind, with the sea a glittering background and the surf singing in the shallows.

After a while, if I sit too long and think, my blood gets sluggish and it is time to move around, to go walking, to restore my balance. So I get up carefully; I have been thinking so long that I have indeed gotten lost and am not sure where exactly to put my first footstep. But somehow I manage to get moving again, to go walking.

Walking along this coast is demanding and exacts attention if you are not to fall over the cliff. It's good to go barefoot, for the feet are starved for stimulation and need the reassurance of rocks and sand—the sharp and the hot—I need the reminder that we are still on solid ground. My feet soak up the heat. I am careful not to break open my skin on sharp stones. If I go barefoot I cannot much moon around for I have to watch the rocks and choose my passage.

Going up the cliff then, early morning, sun shiny on the waves, coast curling to the horizon, big mountains floating on the placid sea, there is a flicker of white. Then the sea breaks open all foamy as the baby whale twirls and twirls under the cliff just beneath me—rising out of the water and looking around, a whirling foam dancer, newborn in the shallows.

That happened one morning. Walking up the cliff, all preoccupied, I reached the top at the exact moment that the baby whale rose out of the transparent water, just where I was looking. I saw her rise up over and over, spinning and twirling around.

I have come not to expect the miraculous—that's a presumption I would avoid—but to understand that these glimpses into a world that exists exquisitely, all around me, are a reward for some effort, choice, and luck. There is no way to see what can be seen from the top of the mountain without climbing; and there is no way to know what is in the water without putting my face into her. So much of my time is spent

15

getting ready, getting in condition, strengthening my body and my mind so that it can go up the mountain or into the sea.

That is the form of life I choose; just as those who wish to see into the world of mind spend much time staring there, so I spend time actually moving myself from place to place, using muscles and organs, active and mobile. And if there is not a piece of cake as dessert, it doesn't much matter, for my blood has flowed freely through me and my back is warm and nourished from my exertions. But it seems often that there is the piece of cake at the turn of the trail or around the coral head; I often find there what I could not find sitting in my living room.

The world of nature is calm and slow moving compared to the world of human mind and human actions. My mind can cycle chaotically and violently for years, overturning personal and social universes, while the sea continues to shine placidly. I am astonished that I can return to the same rock that I sat on three years ago, to overlook the sea, the cliffs, the surf foaming below, and think of all that I have been thinking for all those years—all of the confusion and worry—and still the sea, the sky, the surf remain as I left them.

When I came to the sea, I was tainted with the news for I believed myself to be a newsmaker; and it amazed me that the land was indeed solid, and water wet. Words had come to replace things—it was as if there were no real world, only the spoken or the thought. Especially, too, if the subject is nature, as was mine, so that finally nature becomes symbolic. Rocks stand for ideas, just as whales stand for ideas, or trees or mountain springs. And muddling around in that symbolic world it was easy to cut my feet on the rocks for my mind was floating suspended between yesterday and tomorrow, useless when it came to practical things. I had no knowledge of anything basic: I could not build a fire, I could not loosen a bolt, because my mind and hands had forgotten their essential association, I could not sing in tune because my thought was somewhere else than on melody.

In the midst of all that dreaminess, I came here to look at whales or dolphins and birds, or anything else, still for the most part symbols flopping around in my mind.

So my early training became very explicit. To learn simple things: walking again, sitting, bending, swimming, dancing, singing. To learn to use my body not as a support for a weary mind, but as myself, going along.

This book is my effort of looking and moving. Not at what I dream or think, but at what I see or have seen before me.

Swimming in the shallows, in not more than eight feet of water, along the shore, watching the sand bottom billow up like clouds in the slight surge, I see a *papio,* a flounder, and a *kona* crab, going along the bottom together. The *papio,* silver blue, darting at the turbulence stirred by the crab; the crab, moving slowly, digging around; the flounder, almost invisible, his two eyes staring up from a sand-colored flat body. The three of them going along like that was a humorous and improbable connection: two fish and one crab, looking for food together. Now it is not so improbable, but still charming, for I have seen often, in the shallow water, a young *papio* and a crab gathering food together. But never, since that morning, the flounder with them.

There is no meaning to you of the name *papio* unless you fish these waters; and to look in a book to find the translation would leave you as ignorant as before, only having learned a

17

picture and some words to tell you of a fish that is as mutable and changing as the rainbow, as delicious as life, and strong and fast too.

When I scale a fish, I see its color disappearing before me. The brilliant red of the *menpache* turning dull pink, the scales flying over the sink, the living disappearing. I look at the scales in the sink, and they are colorless, so I don't know where the color has gone. When I scale an *uhu,* the same thing occurs: the iridescent blue shimmer disappears. I noticed this also the time I plucked a newly killed male pheasant to make earrings, I had thought; the bird turned into a naked thing, lost and ugly, where before it had been a beauty, a purple black bronze shin-ing as the smallest feathers disappeared into an anonymous fluff in the glass jar.

I think that a fish and a bird share the same skin, one and the other, feathers and scales. And when the sun shines on the feathery leaves of the ironwood trees, they glisten just like scales; and when he shines on the sandy bottom, the whole shallow sea of the ocean is patterned like a golden fish. I love this correspondence and it charms me.

I remember the particular beauty of my first *papio,* caught on the line, blue fire shimmering, golden eye glaring. And me all caught up in the morning, in the challenge of the fish, the loveliness. It was the first big fish I had ever caught. We rigged a line from the cliff, and I was supposed to get up at dawn to check the line, for if there was a fish, I had to go down the rocks and pull it on shore and carry it—or drag it—up the cliff. I dreaded the morning because I was afraid that I couldn't get the fish in and up, and the cliff looked higher, and the water was pounding and foaming on the rocks.

In the morning there was a fish. I could see from afar that the line was heavy, and there was a flash of silver beneath the foam. I walked along the cliff with a spooky feeling of fear that now I would have to do something I had never done. I couldn't waste the fish, so I went down, hanging onto the cliff, and grabbed at the line swinging in the surf. The water rushed up on the dark rocks; a big silver blue fish was shimmering in the surge.

I grabbed and missed the line, waited for the surge to bring it in again, grabbed and caught it; the wire leader cut into my palm, and I had to let go. I grabbed again, scared and getting a little angry because I couldn't do this thing. But knowing I had to, I took off my T-shirt and wrapped it around my hand and grabbed again, this time hauling in the fish, the big waves breaking around my bare feet. Then, somehow, there was the fish, on the rocks at my feet, shining with all the beauty it is possible to condense in any creature; gleaming blue and yellow gold and silver in the early morning light, and me warming up and excited now, there with the *papio*.

Somehow I went up the cliff, holding on, dragging this fish behind me; it was hard work and scary to get the fish up, even that far. Then I remembered what I had been taught: how to tie the fish on the packframe, tail up, so that the body would not slip, and how to lift him off the ground. I pulled the fish up onto my back and set off down the trail in the early morning sunlight, laughing: alone and laughing, the *papio*'s gold eye glaring behind me.

Now it is raining. The sky is gray and close; rain is splattering down on the big leaves in the garden, the neighbor's dog is barking, and fighting cocks are crowing from their cages. It is a soft gentle rain, the rain that comes in the spring and makes the plants grow, the rain that slows us down and makes sleeping easy. The whales have left these waters for the year, going, I am told, toward the cold places where food is. While I am typing, they are swimming.

As far as I can tell, whales and dolphins, porpoises, swim all the time. When I think of how much I move in my day —and how much they move—I am impressed. I have chased after porpoises on some project or other, maybe thinking we had to take pictures of them, gone off in a powerful boat loaded with stuff (waterproof boxes, cameras, film, hats, sun lotion, recorders, gas, tools, lunch) and with binoculars and glasses found the porpoises swimming freely and calmly over the coral or above the blue sandy bottom. Singing, dancing, hugging each other, moving along like that, they looked slowly in our direction, quickly passed and were gone. And then we swam madly back to the boat, loaded up all our stuff, started the engine, and zoomed around looking for them, caught up with them, and dropped back into the water to watch them go by. Then again they were gone.

After three or four hours of that, we were exhausted and sunburned and confused. But the porpoises go on living as they do, for years and years, day and night, swimming in the ocean of all conditions and all times. Deep dense night of no stars, still swimming in the gentle dark; full moon shining in the water, fish gleaming, phosphorescence in the darkness, still swimming; while I am taking a shower or walking up the long dry mountain, they are swimming, and as I sit here in the ambience of the soft spring rain, watching the beets grow in the garden, I think of them, somewhere, strong swimmers in the south swell.

20

The south swell came up yesterday, and the sea rolled and pounded in. The waves came up over the breakwall, and the harbor was muddy molten. Boats groaned and danced on their creaking lines, and I was too cautious to go swimming.

It is spring, and there is rain in the mountains and hot rolling seas from the south.

You cannot know the absolute power of the weather until you have lived within her provinces. The blurry gray maps that show smudges of clouds covering continents, the bright weary voice reading from the teletype, the natty forecasts after the news, in no way convey the reality of weather for birds, animals, and humans light enough to accept that dominion. The weather determines moods and movement, comfort and misery, calm and anger, food and nuances of delight, and death and birth as well. I do not know when weather stops and something else occurs, when the earth rolls and pitches like a storm wave and spews fire into the night sky; is that still weather or the earth turning in her morning's restlessness? To feel that shaking and rolling under is awesome and exciting, just as watching the great waves come rolling in—the south swell—claims my heart.

All islands have their own weather, and each place is specific and often named for its weather: the sound of its wind or the qualities of a particular rain in the valley. And this weather as surely determines the movements of animals and people as it does the price of real estate. It carves valleys and canyons and impossible impassable mountains out of wind and rain, out of thousands of miles of sea and air mixing. Islands have a windward side and a leeward side. Sometimes they change

21

places as the wind shifts and blows from the other side. Windward is the side the wind blows on. For thousands of miles over the sea and in the high wide blue floating sky, the wind blows, carrying water and freshening it, so that when the rain falls, it is sweet fresh water that flows foaming down the dry streambeds. The rain water flows foaming red brown over the cliffs and tumbles into the sea. And in a big storm the muddy water comes foaming and falling for days and days, the sea water far below turning brown and dense in the great storm, the outlets from the streams shining molten copper in the setting sunlight.

A simple south storm can move immense stones and shake the land for days and days, and carve canyons and build mountains, then pass, leaving a memory and the blush of new green on the hills for the deer to browse.

There is absolute luxury in being an acolyte of the weather, in being free to accept her dominion. I know of no other comfort as lovely as sleeping all afternoon in the warm spring rain; of no luxury so complete as going with the weather, of not fighting it, but traveling with the wind or looking for shade on a hot day; of sleeping in the warm night and waking in the soft wind blowing over the sea—to see the stars as my night companions and see them slowly moving across the soft-spangled dark, sparkling deep velvet, and so far away.

Look across the sea to the mountain, and she too sleeping, and listen to the geckos call at night, and the long waves come rolling in.

The Story
of the Whale
Watchers

This is just a story. Like all stories it is mostly fiction, for the typewriter cannot duplicate experience, and no selection is complete enough to include all of the details, all of the nuances, of real life. The story of the whale watchers can be told as a colorist might tell it, beginning with the exact hue of sunlight, molten silver on the early morning sea, rainbow dazzle coating each wave, as people gather to go out on a boat. It could be told as a story about humans who have expectations and are looking for the next advertised miracle to relieve the assumed boredom of their lives. It could be told as the rocks might tell it, or the cliffs, the long strong presence of the volcanoes, or the sea. So, then, how to tell a story that is not a story of symbol or fantasy, but is a little like what might happen as some people take a journey.

Put yourself, then, in your own place; and look through the photographs, the moving images, the stories, and the songs to where you have, so to speak, arrived. Look around to where you have come, to see what you have never yet seen, but have been promised.

You might begin by looking at the sea. Mutable yet eternal, changing through the day and night, changing color and texture, calm and placid, frothy and white tipped, hissing on the sand, booming in on the cliffs, transparent blue green over the coral, deep milky blue with the sun's rays shining down through the surface, a cathedral, a dancing place. Look at the sea from high up on the mountain, pale silver blue to the horizon, the great islands looking like whales sleeping, the coastline lacy, bays and valleys scallop the shore, the long sweet flank of the mountain furry green in the morning light.

I have looked at the sea through the screen of my own thought and seen something out of focus, glassy, harsh, and having no dimension. I have looked at the sea and seen the shining blue, the pale peaceful volcanoes resting in the haze, and have seen the sea so wild that air and water mixed at the surface, a foaming salty breathing—the sea turned white, as far as I could see, in all directions.

The story of the whale watchers is a story about
a boat going out on the ocean to look for whales—
a sailing ship, once a yacht, now carrying passengers for hire.
The people have seen somewhere an advertisement, a colored picture
which showed them a picture of the boat
a huge whale
rising out of the sea
the creamy white
under her tail
clearly visible
in the picture
and all stopped
eternal
under the blue sky and the shining water.

And so in answer
to the lure of the picture
and words
which promised
the sight of whales
mating
they came a long way
through big booming airplanes
flying in the clouds
drinking liquor
and watching a small screen flicker
with pastel colors of rooms and telephones
and people's faces talking.

They came then
to another place
where the planes roared
in and out
and waited there
for they had brought
special clothing
and cameras
lotions
maps and tickets and
lists of things that were to be done
at a particular time
and there
tucked away
between the white shorts
and the socks
was the picture

of the whale rising out of the sea
shining.

It took a long time
to get everything they had brought with them
and to find a place to sleep
and find food
and lie down
listening to the air conditioners
while the trade winds
blew on the locked windows
carrying the sweet clean air
of the distance they just had traveled.

Trade winds blowing on the locked windows
of the rooms overlooking the sea
and shining out there
in the water
singing
was the whale.

They slept that night
fitfully
for the sound of the air conditioner
was not familiar
and in the broken light of morning
awoke
to the sound of strange birds
cooing and calling
from the trees
outside the windows

and waking there
in the colored light
became conscious
of being where they had gone to.

Listening to the birds coo and call
the soft succulence
the sweet air
that was there
when the people opened the windows
and not too far away
the blue sea
shimmering.

They looked around at the room
pastel flowers on the bedspread
pictures of strange fish
on the walls
the furniture familiar
the soft carpet
the sound of pipes running water
in the next room
and outside the window
the wind blowing
whitecaps
cresting the surface.

The calm sea in the morning
shines like molten silver
and the sun's reflection is a
blinding dazzle

of pure light
shining on the great mirror
the intense bright light
of the sun
seeing himself
in the water.

The people were hungry
for they weren't sure of what to do
and eating was familiar
so they went outside
looking at other people's faces
dislocated
not sure yet
of what they were wearing
for they had bought clothes
specially for the outing
and felt in them
not yet formed
a costume
for the place they had come to.

The food came printed
on a menu
which promised
a variety of similar foods
and they choose
according to the price
or maybe a whim
for the taste of a different fruit
and these came

garnished in orchids
so that it seemed as if indeed
they had traveled somewhere.

A gale is when the winds blow
hard enough
to pick up the sand and dust
and send it flying
so thick it's hard to see
and you walk with your back
to the wind.

A gale is when the winds blow
so hard
that small boats
do not go on the sea
unless protected
by skill and devotion
and a knowledge
of the local waters
and how they act
during a gale.

The radio commonly says
there are small-craft warnings
and gale-force winds
which means
a brisk downwind sail flying
or beating into it
wet and sometimes scared
and sick.

And gales blow often
for they are
the winds of winter and spring
the strong winds
coming from the north
coming from around the corner
cresting the sea
which shines not molten
but now sparkles
and is whitened
by the water foaming
from the top of the waves
as the wind blows them over.

The whales drifted in the deep water
under the cliffs
dark water shining
stars sparkle
the light of a million suns
distant
the quiet blessed night of stars
and the whales drifting
slowly breathing
dozing
in the deep water under the cliffs.

While the people were sleeping
in the room
listening to the air conditioner
the whales were drifting
in the star-filled water

listening to the singing
coming from the fish
and the snails
watching the blur of neon light
as the fish cruised
or slept in their caves
drifting in the water
bodies bobbing in the surge.

While the people were sleeping
and the wind blowing
outside the windows
the deer were resting under the trees
backs to the wind
dark star-filled eyes
glistening.

In the morning the maid comes into the room
and makes the bed
empties the ashtrays
and closing and locking the big glass doors
sprays room freshener
on the carpet and the drapes
and locks the door and leaves
the room humming with the sound of water
running through the pipes
the smell of perfume
settling on the bed.

The people are eating breakfast
in a big room

voluptuous
with immense strange leaves
filling the opened windows
the subtle sound of the surf
hissing on the sand
and metal clinking on glass
the eggs come decorated with flowers
and the cash register is silent
no bell clangs
to count the change
and the paper money
that is exchanged
for the orchids and the eggs.

A big bright blue sky
vaulted overhead
the sea shines and glistens
in the blue early morning light
in the sun's bright light.

While the people were eating breakfast
among the voluptuous leaves
and watching the other people
pass in their unfamiliar clothing
they were dreaming
of something so vastly different
that their senses could not comprehend
and felt only as if
an immense and soothing sleep were upon them
a quietude and a rhythm
significant.

They heard
somewhere deep inside
a great breathing longing
for what was near
yet not present
in the ordinary
shuffling of the eggs
upon the plate
in the vacant looks
exchanged by strangers.

But something trembled there
in the sweet green glossy shadows
between the great leaves
the taro
the banana
the breadfruit
almost perceptible
beckoning
in the breeze.

The trade wind blows
stirring the fallen *plumaria*
the room is comfortable
but something more immense
outside calls.

The people are restless
they have come far
and see each day spent
as costing them something

they cannot afford
and so are eager
for the promised adventure
to begin.

But the ticket they have
is not for this day
so they must find some
other activity
and so they go
to another street
where there are shops that sell
a variety of similar objects
and they are searching
among the goods
for something to ease them
to make them lovely again.

The whales have gone around the corner
up to the point
where the water is turbulent and exciting
to bathe and swim and suckle
in the long afternoon.

The *manini* are drifting in the afternoon tide
grazing the corals
they flash
their yellow green radiance
in the company of each other.

The barracuda drifts lazily

almost motionless
over the coral head
the young hammerhead
flashes her pink-bellied innocence
and looks for food.

Over the water the sky floats
serene and transparently blue
sky of the day.

The people leave the shops
and go then
to look around
on wheels
fast
past the flowers
and the taro
growing in the gardens
past the sweet smile
of the boy on the corner
past bamboo forests
and groves of spiky trees
leaning into the wind
past water falling
into jade green pools
banked by ferns
where lizards dream the day
in the cool crevices.

The people flash by
in tiny identical cars

blurs
of yellow orange and blue
toy cars climbing the mountain.

And the wild goats look mildly down
to the sea
from their caves and ridges
and cannot see
the toy cars
bumping past on the dusty road.

The people
with strained and lost faces
are looking through the windshield
at the unfamiliar road.

The goats are looking
through the portals of heaven
sea and sky
wrapped around them
high on their
mountain
and chewing
the strong bitter grasses
listen
to the wind sing
in the shadows.

The people do not envy the wild goats
their household
for they do not know

who lives there
and see only
the cloud-wreathed ridges
the impossible barren slopes
of the distant mountain
and wonder how far it is
to where they are going.

After a while the people stop
by a sign
and get out of the car
legs cramped
faces flushed and hot
and quickly take pictures
of everything that is around them
and of each other
standing there
the great blue blur of the sea
wavering behind them
the small immaculate flowers
unnoticed at their feet.

And they think then
of a bath and food and drink and
cram themselves
back into the tiny car
and return the way they came.

Wild goats drinking the sweet water
of the mountain
pausing in the late day

to lick each other
to nuzzle and butt
in the sanctity of the shadows
the transparent pools glistening
under the floating leaves.

The next morning
the people dress carefully
for they are going on a boat
to see the whales mating
and the babies playing
as they have been promised
and are hopeful
that the event will be as anticipated
and that they are prepared
with everything they need.

So they carefully select
their costume
and make sure
the camera has enough film
and look through the great glass doors
to see the sea
white and foaming
in the fresh morning wind
and wonder if they will be sick
or get sunburned
and if the boat is safe
and the captain knowledgeable.

And after breakfast

in the big room
banked by the shining leaves
they go quickly to the place
where they will board the boat
for the great adventure
and reaching there
see themselves
in a hundred similar eyes
the hopefulness
the nervousness
the pride.

For they are all strangers
to each other
and to the sea.

And jostle there
seeking shade and comfort
and the best view
but not knowing
from where the vision will come
not yet having seen a whale
except on the small flickering screen
and the importance of the narrator's voice
to tell them
what it is they are seeing.

Some have prepared themselves
with guide books
which show small scratchy pictures
of shapes identified as particular whales

41

of black and white similarity
followed by long foreign names
of species and subspecies.

So even though armed
against the unknown
by all manner of certainties
they are still uncomfortable
under the vast and staring sky.

The people who run the boat
are cheerful
for this is familiar to them
and they have learned
a subtle superiority
to the people
who are strangers
and serve them powdered coffee
in paper cups
with easy joking assurance
and the boat engine
calls her low-pitched roar
as they leave the harbor
for the unknown sea.

Now these people are not a crowd
but a diversity
their uniqueness hidden
under similar clothes
and similar thoughts
for they have all supped

at a common spring of information
and believe exactly
in what they have heard and read
and they all believe themselves knowledgeable
having in their possession
many words of description
for what they have never seen.

The people are anxious then
on this occasion
to display themselves
much like the whales
who often
for no apparent reason
leap out of the sea
and twirl and crash
back into the sounding water
and then again
reach up
their immense water-borne bodies
and fall again
into the welcoming sea.

And to the people this
is a known and labeled event
they have read about
and call
breaching.

The whales were in love
they had come through the vast sounding ocean

come through it since their eyes
first saw the foam
and the mirrored silk of the surface
shining on their birth.

The whales had been in love all their lives
it was their nature
to stroke and nuzzle each other.

From birth
they sang and played
in the warm water
that gave them great cathedrals to dance in
that shone and rippled with the light
splashed out of the lap of the sun
while he flew slowly over the sea
casting rainbow radiance
over the sandy bottom.

The corals shimmered with the colors of fish
who were themselves the colors
of sun shining on corals
and sometimes too
the colors of heaven.

Velvet green and blue
outline the slowly swimming body
of the great male *uhu*
prodding and butting the coral
breaking off from its living face
his breakfast lunch and dinner

slowly floating
day and night
days and nights
and moons and moons and moons
slowly eating the coral
and that's how long too
the whales have been in love.

Hidden by the preoccupation
and the loneliness
the hearts of the people
hungered for love
but they had forgotten
how to speak of it
and spoke only
of ordinary commerce
tried to impress each other
with stories of places
and famous people
they had heard of.

But sometimes the lost love
rose inside unbidden
and they cried
over a story of sadness
like the stories they had heard
about the whales
and their imagined misery.

And thus they recognized
the whales' passion and fruitfulness

and now wished
the whales to unlock their hearts
and let them sing again
to give them something other than currency
to trade with.

The whales knew nothing of this secret longing
heard only the dull thud of the diesel engine
the sound marking the boat as surely
as the name painted on the stern
proclaimed its particular fantasy
to the passengers.

On board the people searched the unfamiliar sea
for unfamiliar signs
of the immensity beneath
and shifted in their seats
restless
uncertain
lost.

The voice of the captain
droned a story
of names and jokes
they could not understand
and the crew
young and bright
with self-importance
preened themselves
in the light
of the people's anxiety.

Then someone shouted
that
a whale could be seen.

The people rushed to the rail
and lifted cameras and binoculars
in front of their eyes
in anticipation
peering through the tiny glass windows
to find the whale.

Then something other
than what they had seen
on the small flickering screen
other than the pictures
in the glossy magazines
rose
foaming
from the deep blue sea
rose immense
and terrifying
shadowing the boat
gleaming darkness
then crashed
back into the water
the sea a wild fountain
soaking the boat
and its passengers
salt spray
running over the lens
blurring the image

and the surface calm again
the sea admitting her own
into her.

The passengers wondering
what it was
that had just happened
the crew
explaining
the action of the whale
words running over the ship
easing the tension
words and light laughter
making the ordinary return
quickly
lest someone hear the sea's great breathing
or notice the paleness flutter
under the boat
where the whale lay resting.

A young girl served drinks
in plastic glasses
to everyone
who drank and joked
and some wound the film in the camera
and looked again to see
where was the whale.

She was singing softly
resting under the boat
listening to the throb of the engine

listening to the muffled clutter
of the humans speaking
about her
and why she had jumped
out of the water.

She was singing to him over there
by the cliff
where he and the others
were slowly gliding
in the light-filled water
slowly sweeping their giant tails
measuring the tune
the air
clinging
outlining their bodies
in rainbow bubbles.

She was singing of the people
and the boat
and listening to the roar
of the distant engine
going away.

She was singing of the star-filled night
and of the great clouds
piling high
over the southern ocean
and of the water
that would soon come
foaming into the sea.

INTERJECTION

This is a comment on the story just told and myself in the telling of it. It has to do with dream and reality and how the two feed and contradict each other. For many of us there is a dream that feeds and sustains us when the matters of the world turn dusty and when nothing we see or hear makes our eyes shine. Then some providence or other causes something to come from deep inside. The old cherished longings for beauty and hope appear; and we, helpless before this inner flood, bestow our dream on something outside of us, idea or person, and follow it as if it were indeed the sun.

It may be the dream of a far-off place, where what occurs will be the answer to our compressed desire, or an idea of this place, transformed back into the garden, the lost place of innocence, where the food tastes fresh upon our lips and is not loaded with confused associations, but comes as it does, fresh from the warm earth, steaming after the summer rain, the blossoms swelling and the leaves full and succulent.

But however it occurs and in whatever guise, it seems we need dreams to excite and sustain us, and our sorrow often comes in the confusion of dream and reality.

So those of us who buy a ticket for the whale dream find that the dream is not purchasable; and it is not a commodity, but a dream; and if we are not careful, we then turn uncertainly to the next notion that might make our eyes shine, just as we turn from lover to lover, hoping that he or she will be the cherished prince or princess.

This seems to be a common process, and one that easily fools us. It makes humans restless and uncertain, and it turns the object of the dream into a possession, a person or thing without qualities, without uniqueness.

So we load onto whale our desire for what is not commonly present in ordinary life, and so loaded, whale is almost obscured by our longing. This probably doesn't much matter to whale, except when it interferes with her life and when she is pushed and exaggerated in order to provide material for a show, in order to confirm the dream.

The story also has to do with our hunger for easy experience, for what is promised as fact by images and print, taken in the comfort of our living rooms. When we watch a TV special on whales, it is not clear that the footage—which seems to take place in that hour—has been gathered over months, and maybe years, and is a compressed vision. Then when we go out to seek similar adventures, we expect that what we will see will duplicate that peculiar fast time of film, that we will witness the spectacular as a matter of course. If we are lucky enough to witness the spectacular we will soon be bored, for we have seen it all before and will wonder restlessly what's coming next.

This hunger for the excitement promised by images urges the people who are contracted to provide the show to indeed provide the show. If you don't see five breaches, each more thrilling than the last, a mating whale, and a mother giving birth, all in the same two-hour boat ride, there is a feeling of disappointment, of loss, of being cheated.

What this has to do with the whales is that it pushes them, over and over, to duplicate a false life, for the whale is not in the water to provide a show for man or woman, but for

51

his or her own reason. And these reasons cannot be found by us if we are full of restless expectation.

So we bind ourselves into a circle of illusion, and, perhaps without wishing, turn the sea into a circus because we have so much desire.

The reality of the whales is something else entirely; it is unimaginable and, for all I know, not perceptible by us. We do not go easily into their world, cannot even breathe its substance. If you really wish to see whales in their world, then you must strengthen and calm yourself enough to go into the water, alone, without fancy gear and without the security of people around you; and then, then you might see whale and understand in your blood and marrow the power of whale and her beauty.

Where
the Whales
Are

Somewhere far north in a colder and crisper sea, the whales are carving canyons and valleys out of shining water and, I am told, catching fish in nets of silver bubbles. It's been a while now since they were here—last spring—and this is midsummer already; so the sense of it is that they won't be back for a while, but will come again this winter, we hope, to give us the excitement of white water fountains, deep booming, crashing, playing, come again to grace this sea.

The last whale anyone saw here was in late May, and that was late; the whales most often come in November or December and leave in March or April. Each year it's like that, the long passage from the Arctic to the mid-Pacific and back: to bear babies and nurse them in the warm water of the semitropical sea; to make love and sing; and then, just as surely, to go north into the cold transparency of the Arctic seas to eat and grow and teach the young.

Whale life is probably much like human life was before human life got hopelessly complicated with things and ideas. I would guess they spend their time in the essentials of moving, eating, finding and avoiding each other, finding food, bearing and nursing babies, and teaching the details of whale life—the intricacies that form their lifelong dance in the sea.

The whales that come here probably descend from a lineage that has existed since the dawn of their time, handing down the knowledge of the route by example and teaching. The ocean is clearly marked by topography, by temperature and current, taste and smell. It's a long passage—thousands of sea miles north and south—but the whales take their time, make their schedule according to the weather, follow the sun and moon, so that the whole northern and central Pacific Ocean becomes an extended home. The shallow warm water in the lee of islands is a place to bear and nurse babies, a court-ing and birthing ground, a nursery and playing place for whales.

I have no idea where whales go in storms or whether it matters to them or whether or not they head for the protection of the lee shore, for it is impossible to see whales in rough seas. A whale breaching or blowing looks just like the foaming, heaving sea. The only time we see whales is in calm weather, which is mostly the only time humans go on the water for fun, for it is no fun beating into a gale unless you are a very particu-lar kind of person. Most often, then, we see whales and they us in the easy shallow sea, close to land, where they go to find the best place to play or to take care of babies.

And so we meet: the big sky gray and hazy with southern clouds, the surface like silver satin, barely rolling. The boat glides, leaving a long wake; on the starboard bow a faint spray, a mist, shows whale breathing.

The sea rolls over and his dark back gleams, a black fan is silhouetted for an instant; then whale sounds, diving deep be-low the surface, the great tail slowly beating, while silver bubbles rise to show his passage. The people on the boat continue to look at the place where the whale sounded, much like we return again and again to the site of excitement, hoping to find it repeated. And so, eyes fixed on the place where he disap- peared, the people do not see whale surface thousands of yards to the north.

The dark back gleams and another, smaller back, rises alongside, and the two whales slowly swim away.

Someone shouts, "There, there," and the people turn to see far in the distance the two dark backs slowly rolling, barely visible in the molten silver sea.

Sometimes watching whales is like watching a comedy. I remember one morning seeing a mother whale nurse her baby in the shallow water just below where I was sitting. I sup- posed she had been there for hours and hours, probably all night, on and off. She looked much like a small island, the sea awash over her glistening back; she hardly moved but drifted on the surface, the water pale turquoise over the baby's white belly. It was a dreamy morning: the sea calm; white-tailed tropic birds riding the updrafts of the cliffs, calling to each other; the mynahs scolding in the *keawe*; and the mother whale nursing her baby in the peaceful sea.

A few small fishing boats returned from dawn trolling and passed the mother without her moving. They were in a hurry to get their fish to the store. The fishermen had seen whales for years and years, so she made no difference to them, and they to her, except maybe they gave her a quick smile of easy recogni- tion. Then came the boats carrying passengers who wished to see something new, and they spotted the mother whale and changed course to have a better look. The mother dove, the baby followed an instant after, and they both disappeared as the boat came near. The boat circled and searched; the people on board looked at the emptiness that had just been whale. She came up a short distance from where she had sounded because the baby couldn't stay under too long. The boat altered course and went toward her. The whales blew—a big misty fountain from the mother, a tiny, barely visible one from the baby—and went under again, the mother first, the baby following. The boat searched the empty sea. I could hear the people on board shouting at the whale, and finding the sea still empty, the boat turned to enter the harbor. The tour boats were on a schedule and couldn't take too long looking. Behind them, in the frothy wake of their prop, the mother and baby surfaced.

The harbor is used by a succession of boats during the day, and for two hours or more, various boats would come into the entrance, spot the mother whale, and go searching for her; and she, in turn, would disappear with her baby below the surface. After a time, the mother, probably realizing that she couldn't nurse, surfaced and headed slowly up the coast, away from the complication of boats and people.

This curiosity about mother and baby whales is hard on them because there are only so many days and nights before she and the baby must leave to make the long passage north. If she is constantly interrupted by the curious, then she cannot physically pour enough milk into her infant to get him or her in good strong condition to travel with her and weather the cold water of their first year in the Arctic.

It would be useless to try to put the whales on a map by drawing a neat outline of the coast, with an X marked for each whale. Whales are not on paper, they are in water. They are not stationary, they are moving; and they move in relation to wind and weather, to the events of their days and nights, and will not hold still for mapping or easy diagrams.

What will determine the location of whales is weather, which follows its own schedule and cannot be predicted, no matter how fancy the computer, no matter how smart the fore-caster. The only thing you can do is to learn to read the imme-diate signs and sounds and smells of coming and changing weather, and to know something of local patterns, which, if you are attentive and not too theoretical, can inform you of the coming day. But you can listen to the voice on the radio tell you of light and variable winds on the stretch of coast you are watching; and even as the voice talks, you see the horizon turn white and hazy from the force of a gale.

And it will matter, too, if it is a weekday or a weekend and what humans are doing at the time and whether they and the whales are consonant or at odds and whether the whales wish to be left alone or are in the mood to play.

It seems that the whales who are interested in people are the ones who do not have young to protect or care for. Adoles-cents born in these waters and used to the sound of boats and the coming and going of the curious, who have learned not to fear humans and who have time and energy for fooling around, seem to be the ones who might swim to us and say hello.

The question then is whether you have the energy and time to swim to them and say hello.

Whales' House

People here call

an octopus a squid. I don't know why they do, for they know the difference between squid and octopus more surely than I. But when they go to hunt for octopus in his holes in the coral reef, they say they are going squidding; and when they catch octopus, they call it squid. Just the same way that I have the habit of calling a dolphin a porpoise, or a porpoise a dolphin, using the word more for its sound in the sentence than for its accuracy of description, for I have never yet gotten straight the difference between dolphins and porpoises, except that, I think, dolphins are bigger and have different noses. Anyway, the dolphins most often seen here are porpoises, but sometimes they are bigger and are, I guess, dolphins; so bear with us in our refusal to name an octopus an octopus.

Once ink came from the octopus, and it still does. When the octopus is disturbed in his house, he spits out a mess of dark brown murky ink, which hides him from you who are looking. There is something surely awesome in this clouding of the water around the house of the octopus.

I once put the ink from the octopus in the cooler, trying to save it, thinking I might return to the simplicity of a feather dipped in octopus ink as a slower and more graceful way of writing. But my habits are vastly lazy, and the ink turned foul smelling and rotten; and I had to throw it out because I was inattentive.

The word *sepia,* I think, once described the color of octopus ink on paper. It is a graceful and quiet color, that shade of soft brown on the page. I think of those early naturalists, feathers dipped in octopus ink, sitting in the shade of the banyan tree, carefully drawing the details of a newly discovered —to them—leaf.

If you are wondering what octopus ink has to do with the location or habits of whales, it might be more correspondent than you think, for they share the same world and live in proximity and association; and there is no way to know what their conversation might be—for, indeed, it might occur.

I am amused that the idea of ecology, which once meant to learn about the household, came into our minds as an organizational chart shaped like a pyramid with man at the top. It hardly matters, but if I wish to talk about the ecology of whales as something to do with whale and octopus sharing the same household, people are not used to thinking that that is ecology.

Yet just as land animals and plants breathe and share a common air and recirculate it for each other, so whales and octopus, or squid, share a common sea with corals and fish and recirculate it for each other.

If you breathe the air just next to the surface of the sea, especially if it is stormy, it is salty. The spray and foam carry salt and throw it bubbling on the rocks to form salt ponds, which are suitable for salting and preserving the octopus.

Once I went swimming under a waterfall. The storm rains had created a roaring of white spray and falling water where there had been only a dry stone riverbed the day before, and we, delighted with this new toy, went playing under the cascading water. The water pouring over the falls was so sweet and tempting that I had to hold myself back from breathing it in in great lungfuls. Some chemistry or physics of water in motion gave to the falling water a smell and taste of such seductiveness that it took conscious effort not to breathe it in.

Not too long ago I sat on the beach and watched the mist rising from the sea into the sky, and I realized that I was actually seeing a cloud form, that it wasn't just an idea for a school test. Water did, in fact, steam up from the surface of the sea, steam in the heat of the sun, and gather in the air as a great misty curtain, a vast pearly haze rising off the ocean forming clouds. Then, not too long after, in the south I saw miles and miles of blue gray mist falling, as rain, back into the sea, not very distant from where it had risen—a hydrological cycle had come alive, the story of water rising and falling, salt and fresh, continually.

I sit in that amphitheater of wonder and watch clouds forming and dissolving over the sea, under the vault of sky, the immensity, the long blue horizon, the color and the warmth.

So this household of whales—their ecology—is where whale and dolphin and jellyfish and squid live together over immeasurable distance of shifting water, for there is hardly a way to measure inches of something that is flowing, drifting, and roaring. So there is no way to say the dimensions of the whales' house unless we measure by some landmark, just as waters are named for land and sometimes for their qualities.

The English language has words for water: there are sea, ocean, river, brook, stream, lake, pond, rain, mist, steam, cloud, waterfall. These words describe the container of land for the water, or maybe a way the water goes, or a dimension. The words seem to describe something seen from outside, as a flowing brook is seen in a landscape painting, but not as from inside, from living in the water of the brook, or being the water of the brook.

Then go inside whales' house, go into the water, or more accurately, float and play on the surface, looking down, as from the sky, on the animals of the water and their colors and movement and ways of being with each other; see the layered light and the sun shining silver blue through the surface.

On a ship at sea, five days away from land, I looked at the sunset sky with great attention for there was only the sea and the sky and the ship to interest me. I watched the glory of the full sea sky turn all the colors of sunlight, blazing and glowing with red gold light; and after all that passion and beauty, I watched the colors fade into blue and gray, and after a long long time, turn dark blue black and show stars shining. And, at the time, I wondered if the whales, too, look at the sun setting, the immense blazing fire going away, and if the whales feel the loss of loveliness and then feel, too, the slow return of beauty—the stars' deep dazzling peace.

Whether or not whales in their house contain that dimension—the appreciation of beauty and the sadness of its loss—is something to wonder about, for it must be that animals see and appreciate beauty. There is no other way to explain to me the velvet antlers of the deer or the iridescent loveliness of the male pheasant.

Nowadays humans select each other mostly for possessions, or their potential for possessions; but animals are honest in their appreciation of strength and beauty, casting it before them as a carpet into the future, making the pheasant's feathers ever more and more shining, as lady pheasants time and time again fall for the dazzle. And now when I look at most humans, especially the possession-centered ones, their bodies seem mere appendages to carry things on, and have lost their suppleness, usefulness, and grace.

But in whales' house there is little to possess, and there is much intrinsic beauty. There is a God-given loveliness of surrounding, which may form part of whale and octopus dreams, and certainly does form their seascape. Their house is, so to speak, decorated with each other.

Playing Around
with Whale

The sea is a perfect playground—sometimes calm and inviting, other times a playground for the strong and blessed—when she is herself playing. A lady I know says the gods are angry—*akua huhu*—when the wind blows wild and strong and the sea roars and the gigantic foaming, hissing waves come rolling in. Maybe the sea is just playing, but like any strong animal, rough when she plays.

I have no idea if the sea has moods, but she surely follows the moon, for I see that. The water comes higher on the land when the moon is full, and then comes high again when the new moon brightens the western sky. The fish follow the tide line and come in when the moon is full and its big blue silver light shines through the water. It used to be, I think, that women followed the moon with their rain, their birth blood, but now that's tangled with electricity. And animals follow the moon, the deer and goats browsing the nights of moonlight, the mouse about, the owl hunting; and we all sleep better in the dark. Plants, too, follow the moon, and the best time to plant is when the moon shines into the hole dug for the seed.

So this vast expanse of moving water, the sea, is following the pull of the moon and her light; and all of the creatures that live in her are following the same rhythm. The great cosmic beat changes about every six hours as the tides change; the sea pulls out, then comes in again, pounding into the cliffs, over-running the tide pools, foaming over the wet black rocks, triumphant or, at least, frisky.

Yesterday my dog chased my young horse around the corral three times, very fast. I loved seeing her race by, free and flowing, and then when she reached me, she turned and kicked high, pranced in front of me to make sure I was taking note. I think it was because I wouldn't let her eat my ukulele or maybe because I tapped her on the nose and said no. There she was off and running, and breathtakingly beautiful and frisky—playing.

When my horse came charging at me, full of her impatience at my slow bumbling, I stepped aside because I did not want to risk her thundering down on me. Then I spent a sleepless night thinking I had no courage or faith—in myself, nor in her. I am still not sure whether I was a coward or prudent, but certainly I was not strong or fast enough to play with her on her ground. My dog, who is small and short, is very fast and agile, so that even though he is lacking in size, he can play with the filly, whereas I can only watch.

My horse and I are not so different in size. Consider how much bigger is the sea or whale.

If one could only go into the sea as a baby, but with full strong ability to stay easily in the deep water far from shore, then one could go into the sea not as a problem, but as a playground, and watch the light and listen to the soft static clicking of the shrimp and fish and the soft breathing of the water.

Look at the colors of the corals, their flowerlike forms still and silent in the shifting underwater light. The fish are prodding and probing, turning silver and gold as they flash and flare their breathing scales and reflect the sun. The *manini* are pale yellow green striped with a smoky brown, marked just like the yellow coral they graze upon; a great cloud of them, hundreds and hundreds, drift and graze in the surf's surge. They look like filtered striped light, the same light that shines, without them, on the yellow green coral.

If you make your mind very silent and stop talking to yourself, you can hear the soft electric sound of the *uhu*—parrotfish—banging the coral with his nose, breaking away his dinner. I read in a book that some *uhu* are born females; when they are young, they are brown, reddish brown, or soft gray. As they get older, become bigger, and turn into males, their color changes from reddish brown to cobalt blue or iridescent lavender. A big *uhu* is one of the loveliest of God's creatures, and, if the book is accurate, remembers himself as a female once. But I have never seen anything like an *uhu* changing her sex and color; I repeat it only as a curious notion.

Two days ago a boy drowned in the sea because he was playing and was not strong enough or wise enough or blessed enough to come back to land. There are many stories that try to fix the blame of it on something or somebody—and the boy is hardly lost yet, but already the stories are strong and complex. The place where he drowned is a leaping-off place; a ledge juts out over the deep water directly below, and the sea rushes foaming and fast up over the rocks, and then sucks out fast, cascading water. The place is turbulent and risky when the sea is rough.

It's a place I have often seen whales, near Pu'upehe, an ancient shrine: a lovely place, a strong place to leave your spirit. And as we are all trying to insure against death by some act or other of knowledge or attitude, it is possible to think of that place and that boy as married now, by story, to each other. Yet I have no idea if the sea noticed the drowning boy or if she notices the crying fish fighting on the line.

Today I went swimming because I didn't want to burden my mind with doubt or fear, but I did not go to the place where the boy drowned because it didn't seem proper to go there now. The sky is heavy with clouds and rain waiting to fall; the air is heavy and dense with the coming water. The sea is rough in the path of the trade winds and calm in the lee of the mountain. The boy has been taken from the sea and given over to the rituals of the land. The whales are somewhere north of here, and I would imagine they are playing. I have never played with whales in the water, and have only seen them playing on the surface, but their play is monumental.

It's easy to get confused about the size of whale because for most people whale is an image, not a presence. And viewing that image, a picture held in your hand or a TV screen that you can easily carry in your arms, would not remind you that whale is enormous. And being in the presence of enormous in his or her house is, to say the least, awesome. Looking over or down from a big boat is also confusing for then the size of the boat becomes human's house, and humans become that size, so to speak, in the presence of whale.

Slip from the boat and the image into the water, into the substance of whale's house, and watch him or her slowly approach. Watch even a small porpoise swim up very fast, and so easily, directly toward you, wanting to play.

I remember once swimming out to see the porps. They had been fooling around Manele Bay for hours, coming close

74

inside; so I decided if I went out, I might see them, and went out, and did see them, many of them, ghosting past, swimming that slow rhythmical beat they swim, a kind of keeping time, a pulsing. I found that porpoise who often has something she carries to play with: a piece of plastic bag, a piece of seaweed. Seeing her there I decided to try to play with her: kind of silly, me with no ability, just a pair of swim fins, a snorkel and mask, trying to keep up with an adult porpoise. I was sure it was a she, yet nothing but intuition told me so; and offering her in my awkward clumsy way a piece of seaweed—*limu*—as a plaything, I tried to swim fast enough to interest her in me and in this toy. Good fun it was, and she, too, was interested in me. I was all alone and no threat; there were fifty or so porpoises nearby. We played around with one another; I trying to catch up and hand her the *limu,* and she, looking at me with her great grave brown eye, coming back and circling around.

Then I found I was very far out, and the porps were going even farther out, so it was time to acknowledge that I was of the land and not of the sea and turn back. Just as I turned, I saw what at first seemed another porp, almost motionless on the bottom, lying on the sand, nearly the same size and color as a porp. But I knew that it couldn't be a porp because they don't stay on the bottom like that. It must be a shark, and the word flooded my mind with fear. I wondered what to do, alone and far out; the porps were heading out even more, leaving me and the shark.

There was nothing to do but to swim quietly and carefully home. I turned away from the shark and headed shoreward. Then I remembered that I shouldn't turn my back on the shark, so changed direction and followed him. He was still swimming gracefully and quietly on the bottom. Finally he disappeared into the blue-filtered deep, and I turned and stroked for shore.

I knew there was no room for panic and shouting, for it would be useless, but my blood was flowing strong and sure through my veins, and my body was responsive and alive with the strong pulsing of my heart. I swam like a gold-medal winner, like I never had before, back to the beach, so much power and strength in me. When I reached the shore and rose out of the water and looked at the people there, ordinary and happy enough, I felt eight feet tall, like a queen rising from the blue. And the shark himself was no menace, he had never even bothered me; it was the fear, in a real context, that had given me that power.

I knew then the difference between imaginary fear—the kind given by image or story, the kind that leaves me limp and sad; and reality, the kind that allows my body a way to respond. That natural juice, all stored up by a nature that knew her business, came to me so I could swim like that, strong and sure, and reach the shore. And the shark never even bothered, only kept going his way as if I had not even been there.

I told the story to my friend and fishing partner, and told it with a cocky turn of voice, as if there had never been anything to worry about in the water. I was told that I was stupid and had not yet enough experience to know that the sea always must be respected.

After the argument that came, I thought about what my friend had said; and now when I enter the ocean, I pray for my loved ones and that the grace of the sea be in me and that I have a good swim. And I think of that now, on this rainy foggy night, with the sea roaring in her pride and the whole town feeling the loss of the drowned boy.

Animals are physical; their strength, power, and intelligence are concentrated in their bodies' abilities. They live in direct and intimate contact with the things, smells, and textures of this world—earth or water. Their information about each other and their surroundings comes directly into them, without explanation. Animals do not seem to be much confused, unless they are unfortunate and come under the dominion of a confused human, who can easily distort their world enough to make it chaotic—much as we ourselves distort our world by thought and action until it hardly fits the human hand anymore, let alone the human heart.

Animals left on their own are perfectly adapted and qualified to find their way and to know what is happening around them. What my baby horse has in common with a baby whale is a considerable amount of similar energy, curiosity, and physicality. The nostrils of my baby horse look just like a whale's blowhole, and she has a goofy way of putting her head under water and splashing in the water trough that is very whale-like. Her curiosity about the world and her way of being with her mother are similar to what I have seen in baby whales. Often now it seems that my horse nurses not so much for the milk, for she is eating grass and grain, but for the reassurance. So that just after tossing herself in front of me and kicking up her legs in a spirited show of strength and independence, she runs over to her mother and suckles for a while to show me, I guess, that I am not her mother and that she is protected. Just as the mother horse is an island of security in the pasture, so is the whale mother an island of security in the sea.

Whales have always seemed essentially remote and inaccessible. The first time I saw a whale, I was in a little gray rubber boat with several young men. The outboard engine was whining, the long sandbanks of the Mexican desert all around; and one of the young men was standing up in the boat, full of his authority to have the best view, taking pictures of the rolling turning whale, while the other young men were eager to go on with the chase. My heart saddened, and all I wished was that we would turn away and leave what we had come so far to see.

That feeling of being an intruder comes often when I am on a boat with people who are chasing a whale. But it does not come at night on a small boat in the starlit darkness. Then to have a big whale, or two or three surface very close, from unknown quarters, and blow that breath that is the greatest sound of breathing I have ever heard, like hearing the sea herself release her breath. I feel nervous and a little scared of the dark immensity, of the effortless back quietly rolling the dark sea over. Often on nights with whales around I would shout and laugh self-consciously, wishing to be sure that they heard us, that they would not in some inattention run us over.

Approaching my horse, I hold out my open hand to her so that she might take my smell. I touch the soft velvet of her delicate nose and see her baby whale nostrils opening and nuzzling. But with the whales or dolphins my hands seem so meager, and we are not animals sharing the same scent. With them, my open hand seems intrusive, except for the time I swam after the porp to offer her a piece of *limu*.

I have never tried to swim after a dolphin to touch him. The dolphins touch often, they hold onto each other, hugging as they beat and flex their way through the long slow days and nights of their lives. I have seen them thus, bellies together, brown eyes gazing my way as I float about them.

78

I reflect on how arrogant it is to assume to be the protector of a whale or a mountain—a kind of possession by default—as if we could, with any strength of our own, take care of anything that much bigger than we are, as if, indeed, it were not the other way around, that the mountain takes care of me and allows me to put foot on stone and dirt and gives me the warm earth for a bed and the sweet grass for a pillow. I noticed that when my eyes centered on the typewriter, it was possible to construct all manner of impossible worlds, such as a person saving a whale, particularly lamentable because the person could not even swim, and had to buy food from the store. I had lost even the simplest abilities, but embroidered mentation until it was possible to construct such an absurdity as saving a whale. And then sometime later, while I was sitting on the shore of the warm salty sea, I laughed at my immense presumption, at the absurdity of the vision.

Going from the desk to the sea, I was so unable, so useless, that indeed it would be the whale who might save me, if one ever considered that a possible action; finding that whale was real and water was deep, while big fish or unknown attitude cruised by, looking at home there, residential in the sea. And ever since then, as an author of reputation, I find a great distrust of the written word rising up, as big as any whale, as wide as the sky arches around. Then, planted in this paradox, I remember what the word *error* once meant—to wander—much as the knights errant wandered in search of loveliness.

Some summers ago we camped at Kaunolu, a sacred place where a stream flowed down to the sea and where, on the side of its once-living banks, some people long ago had constructed a temple. Separated from the cliff of the temple by a narrow

79

gap was a spire of lava rock, a natural tower or monument, which was the landing place of man.

Fishing from the cliff across the streambed from the temple, we looked down on the current swirling the foam sea —white flecks of air and water that tell of the turbulence beneath. We looked down to see a river of peacock blue, silver gold *papio* swimming along the cliff very fast; there were sixty or so very big, exquisite fish running under us, then turning and flashing back the way they came, so brilliant they were a present from that place that honored us that day.

Not too much later, we looked in the current to see two big rays fluttering their wings over each other, the sound clearly reaching us, the excitement and the pleasure of the two big rays making love on a summer day.

The same weekend I climbed down and across and up the streambed and walked carefully across the rocks of the temple, asking my leave for being there, to reach a place where the rock of the ledge gives way in one great natural gap to a place where you can leap into the sea, a long way down, the water deep, cool and inviting under the gap, and saw down there, swimming fast in the transparent green water, six sharks, gray and sleek, playing.

As I looked at the sharks from above, they seemed as lovely as the porpoises, as fast and graceful, only their fierce reputation volunteering fear.

I remember that day as expressive of the fecundity of summer: the *papio,* the rays, the sharks, the landing place of man.

Whale Song

Long before you

see them, you can hear them—the gentle soft clicking of the dolphins, the drawn eerie crying of the whales. If the water is murky, you may not see whales or porps, or anything, until they are quite close, twenty or thirty feet sometimes, but you may hear them calling and singing thousands of yards away. Often your first awareness that the porps are present is the light wash of sound coming from somewhere; and heading into that sound, swimming after it, you find in the dusty blue water the first ghost shape swimming by, then resolving in the dim light, the whole gathering of porps drifting past in twos and threes, unfolding their quiet grace, singing, and clicking.

The sea is not silent, but soft. Her music rolls gently, surrounding rather than bombarding. In order to hear the music the sea sings, you must stop your thought from filling your head with its noises and turn yourself to listening instead.

The dolphins sing and talk, and are also silent. Their sound washes you with a gentle clicking, a humming, and purring. The song whale sings is stronger, sometimes very funny, all of the farting and belching and roaring sounds of the land, but on a vast scale, floating in the filtered sea.

The dolphin's song changes. I heard them once in the deep blue water over the sand at the entrance to the harbor. It is a place they often come in the early morning to rest and play, swimming long lazy loops and circles in the calm water, and singing. We were watching them, floating with them—easy and lazy, the dolphs and we—and they were singing and clicking and lazying around. Then the song changed. It was a distinct change, very noticeable; and as the song changed, so did their movements, which went from long easy looping lines to a coming together from all over. Suddenly the whole bunch converged and spiraled in a swirling curve down to the bottom, a great cone of swirling dolphins singing in the morning.

Sometimes when swimming around dolphs I call or sing in my snorkel, kind of coaxingly, to let them know the sound of my voice, to try to form some bond of recognition.

The song of the calm inshore water is a soft clicking, so fine and soft you must be very silent inside to hear it. I am told it is the shrimps clicking their claws together, calling each other and, for all I know, calling me.

I have never heard the fish singing. I have heard them on land, crying or croaking, but in the sea, swimming with the *manini,* the *uhu,* the *weke,* I can hear only the soft clicking of the shrimps and, if I am very silent, the barely perceptible thud of the *uhu* as she bangs the coral to loosen it with her mouth. But to hear the *uhu* banging the coral, you have to be very quiet indeed, and there can be no interference from your mind's voice talking inside.

In order to hear, you must learn to listen, which is a way of making yourself transparent to outside sounds so they can come in and find residence inside. It is much like learning a new tune, like singing on key.

When you swim on the surface, it is easy to hear the sound of a boat's engine coming or going—the high whine of an outboard or the low roar of a diesel. I am sure the whales recognize, by sound, all of the boats common in these waters.

Sometimes people on a boat will yell and whistle at whales, and maybe the whales hear them. I know one lady who is sure that they come when she shouts at them.

Each place has its song: the sound of the inshore water, the sound of the deep blue sea, the sea calm and the sea passionate, hissing and roaring. The sound of the great waves booming in on the sand is different from the sound they make when crashing on rock and coral, and it is possible, waking in the night, to know when the surf comes up from the changing sound, to know at what exact moment the sea is lifting and coming in strong and to know from what direction—the deep echoing roaring under the cliffs or the hollow booming in on the sand in the bay.

And if my thought-filled ears can learn to hear, I marvel at the intentness of the dolphin, of the deer. Watching the deer resting under the *keawe* in the hot noonday sun, flies buzzing, I see their ears swivel and turn, alert to the changing sounds on the mountain, pointy and mobile, the deer's ears. My dog sees or hears the deer from a long way away, and his look changes. His panting mouth closes, the sound of his breathing stops, his ears point, he is all stillness and expectancy. I look in the direction he is looking and see the slight flicker of white in the dry *koa*— the two fawns passing.

At midday in the ironwood forest we listen to the singing of the trees in the wind, the fallen needles soft and warm. The forest offers deer and humans a place to rest in the shade, a place to pass the long hot hours. The wind rustles through the silky feathery leaves, and the sun shines on them, refracting rainbow light like on scales and hair.

The *keawe* forest groans and creaks in the wind, and branches rub against one another, sounding like people calling or singing. Sometimes when I'm alone at night, listening to the *keawe* forest is spooky; there is too much presence there for restful sleep.

Nothing is as duplicated, and for a long time I believed I was hearing whales singing when I listened to a recording. Then I heard something in the sea, and it didn't sound like the recording. It was different; I wasn't in my living room; I was in the water—listening.

Sometimes when my mind is talking too much, I stop to listen to the song the trees sing, or to the shrimp clicking under the boat, or I watch the crab dig backwards down into the sand, disappearing fast in a little pouf of sand, leaving only two iridescent spots—his eyes—still looking at me while the *papio* stays above him, waiting for him to come out again so they can go foraging.

The Art
of Looking

When I was eight years old, the teacher, a discoverer of imperfections, found that the reason I didn't pay attention in school was that I could not read the blackboard. It might actually have been that my desire drifted outside and that my young blood wished to stir like the filly on a windy day, more than to concentrate on the intricacies of multiplication. At any rate it was because I could not see, or could not see well enough to satisfy my teacher's exacting standards of attention. So I was sent out for glasses, and for a long time of buried agony, adjusted, or did not, to the ugly things—heavy and always getting lost—and I, at eight, was lost enough as it was, without having to add to the indignity. Since then I have looked at the world mostly through progressively stronger glasses, for what in that system could possibly help my eyes, which probably wished only to feast on green and to watch the fuzzy clouds change form and sail over the mountain. If there is anything that does not have to be seen sharply delineated, glassy, and peculiarly flat, it's clouds.

Now when I take off my glasses and look at the pasture or the sea or the clouds floating, the world comes soft and gentle to me, easier, as my eyes rest from the immense chore of seeing sharply. And people's faces, too, are gentler, the expression less distinct. This is a great advantage, to my ease of mind, for I do not have to wonder so much about everyone else, and can smile blankly at the person I see standing there in the coconut-dappled shadows, so surely handsome and reminding me of Gauguin's paintings of pink sandy beaches and lavender mountains; and palm trees, leaves like flight feathers of big birds, sounding like rain, rustling in the breeze. I see the person, then, in perspective, so to say, and of the proper intensity. But if I look at people with my glasses on, they become larger than the palm, of greater interest than the mountain, which is much bigger and gives a radiating calm.

Glasses, then, are for sharp focus and headaches, and for making lines form on my forehead and stiffness in my neck from the effort of holding them in place so that they won't slip down my nose or slide into the water. And if that is not enough, I somehow convinced myself that I needed to see sharply in the sea, so I now have a mask that makes black rings around my eyes because of the rotting rubber that presses against my forehead and binds against my head, all in an effort to see sharply.

Opening my eyes underwater without a mask washes them and salts them with a fluid almost exactly like the one the doctor gave me for washing my eyes, sterilized and in a small plastic bottle. Does the sea have germs?

Yesterday a great yellow brown green scuzz drifted in on the water, dusting the surface. Sitting on the sand and looking at the scuzz floating in, we had a learned conversation about what it could be. Many of those present had degrees in science from universities, but very bad eyes; and it was almost impossible to tell, from looking, what was floating on the water.

None of us wished to go too close to the scuzz for fear of getting dirty, so we were, indeed, mystified by it, but we could
discuss easily enough what it might be.

Each person has his or her own focus, that place where our
eyes join an image that is clear for us, so we might be, I guess,
professors of our own focal distance, experts in the description
of something close, or far, or vivid green and blue. Altogether,
then, if we could share our vision, we would have a composite
view of the sea and the mountain, of the scuzz. Instead, each
of us wishes to be the one holding the perfect knowledge, the
20/20 vision; so description becomes argument rather than the
layering of successive and simultaneous images one upon the
other.

We decided yesterday on the beach that what makes us
educated isn't that we know very much, but that we can talk
easily about what we don't know.

There is a succession of subtle shadings that transmute day
into night and back into day, and a day and a night paid exact
attention to might be an eternity. There is no moment that one
begins or ends; there is no precise instant the day starts or
ends. It does not start at dawn, but subtly, long before, in the
gradual changing of the darkness. It does not end with sunset,
for after sunset is the changing of color from cold gray back
into radiant pink and gold again. When night settles, the first
star has shown itself long before; and the moon shows palely
beautiful in the daylight; then the golden full moon rising between the islands comes again on the water.

There is a golden pathway, a reflection of the moon's and
sun's light on the sea, glistening and immensely lovely, as the
full moon rises in the summer.

With my glasses on I see one moon with a sharp edge around her, markings clearly visible; without my glasses I see a moon that is a five-petaled flower, glowing, misty around the edges, pulsing and moving. With my glasses on hardly anything moves in my vision; everything appears still and sharp and flat. Without them I see colors and big soft fluffy clouds floating in a pale blue sky that is airy and very far above; and to see all this I must lift my head and bend my neck backwards and stretch my body.

I once met a lady sitting in a jeep on the sand while two hundred yards from her, in the strong wind, a number of people were salvaging a stranded schooner from the water of the reef, going back and forth with pieces of the stricken ship. A pretty ship she was—green and white—leaning heavily over, her deck almost at right angles to the water, the coral underfoot, the wind gusting, and the schooner shaking. Pieces of her were being cut and sawed and pulled out and carried to shore to be put in a heap, just a little way from this lady in the jeep, who was reading a romantic novel of south sea adventures —about the place where we were, actually, at that moment, salvaging the schooner. The lady read on, too absorbed to even notice.

It truly amazed me that her focus could be so print-sized when all around were the dimensions of sea and mountain, of far-off islands, of foaming water, and the invitation to participate. When her brother had finished taking pictures of the picturesque schooner and of us carrying all this stuff over the reef, he got into the jeep while the lady went on reading; and they drove away on the sand, back to the city they had come from.

I spent hours and hours and days and days of my young life lying on my back in a sun-filled porch, my feet propped up on a red leather armchair, holding a book over my head like the sky, reading of mistreated things, of far-off time, and of universes so big you could get lost in them. Just next to the house a stream flowed, which was frozen in winter, a skating place where we could skate around the boulders, and in summer peer into the warm greenish water. Never in that time that I remember did I connect the book with the stream.

Now when I read of streams, they do not seem like streams, but like descriptions I have read before, successions of words claiming my attention.

But to look at stream, to listen to stream, to feel her warmth or cold or touch her margins or her deeps; no, I don't know stream; mostly I sit by stream and think, and think about my stiff neck and why I cannot move like my horse, or my dog, or the dolphins.

The very first time I ever went hunting was in a valley that had been carved by the wind and rain into an awesome and practically impassable landscape. We camped on the floor of the valley, set up our tent, and built a fire under the shadow of the mountain we would climb the next day. We looked at the tiny black dots on the high horizon—goats or boulders, there was no way to be sure. In the morning my friend, who is a true hunter, an animal himself, took his bow and arrows and went up the mountain to look for the black dots. I waited around camp, far more interested in drinking coffee and combing my hair than in goat hunting, a little bit afraid of the vast landscape. An hour later my friend returned, surprised that I was still dawdling over the coffee and the comb, and told me

93

to get going and follow him. Being trained as I am by magazines and pictures, the question of my hunting costume con-
sumed me, for I wanted to look good, to look like I was actually doing it: hunting. So after some more fussing with myself,
rearranging my hunting image to suit my inner eye, self-
consciously and very pleased with myself, I took up my bow
and arrows, more decoration or prop than weapon or tool, and
set up the trail to the mountain. I mooned around, looking at
this or that—the glistening sea, the small flowers, the sky
—very taken with myself as a hunter, and in a short time
scared a herd of goats, who all ran before me in a flurry, charming and self-possessed on the stony ground. I was very surprised and even more pleased with myself for having found the
goats so easily and thought it a pity that my friend, the hunter,
was not there to see the herd I had found for him. Then, lifting
myself from my reverie, I saw him a bare twenty yards ahead
of me, waving his arms and shouting at me in a fury; I had, in
fact, scared the herd he had been stalking with great care for
almost an hour. After his temper cooled, he asked me why I
had not been looking around, for I was in the hunting ground.
He told me that he had frantically been trying to wave me
back from the path for the full fifteen minutes he had seen me
dawdling up the trail. Was I not looking, he demanded, was I
not looking?

Well, I was looking. I was looking at my inner dream of
myself as a bow hunter, climbing up the mountain in the
morning, appropriately dressed, with my splendid bow ready,
just like in the movies. But as for looking outward, looking at
what was around me, or even noticing my friend waving from
behind the rock outcrop, that focus had never occurred to me.
It was something about not knowing when to begin, not un-

derstanding the purest basic about hunting, which was simply to look, to look out all around, to move slowly with surety. It was not the time to take a stroll up the mountain.

Hunting is instructive to me, for it shows me myself more surely than any mirror. It shows me my preoccupation with what is not around me, my peculiar city innocence of surroundings. It shows me my intense preoccupation with self-image.

Looking with eyes open and not prefocused, or looking inwardly at self-looking, is not practiced too much by people raised on images and self-images. If you wish to travel to see something, such as whales or dolphins or the empty silent sea shining in the path of the moon's light, it takes a certain relaxation of habit. It takes a new form of attention, so that returning, you are not left with an empty bank of self-images, but have stored for life those flickers of life seen and lived differently.

Someone once said to me there is no such thing as time wasted in life; all life is lived and that is that. Perhaps. But when I think of how little enters when I am self-occupied, then it seems, indeed, as if my life was spent largely in a dream. It was as if I were sitting always by the flowing stream, dreaming of myself sitting there, and more surely out of touch with the coldness of the water, or the green iridescent flash of a resident, than if I were still encapsulated on my adolescent porch, lost in descriptions of worlds beyond worlds, while just outside, the live stream called and sparkled, as far away as the cosmos, as far away as the Sahara Desert or the sleek black horse I ran with in my dreams.

This is no crime, but only a description of a loss of senses —a loss so nearly complete in adulthood that when I watch the dolphins swing their gentle eyes toward me in the dappled sun-filled water or when my filly runs in the dew-wet grass in answer to her sweet inner urge to be alive, I cannot imagine what to do except think and explain and ponder and get lost in description.

So what, then, is looking but letting the outside in again and letting my intense gaze fall silent and open so that what is there might enter, as a guest in my house, as something bidden in by my desire not to dream away this life. I do not want to stare blankly at myself walking up the mountain, bow in hand, not seeing the goats standing there looking down at me—a hunter they could not possibly take seriously because I had not the most basic ability to see.

The irony was that we returned from the goat hunt not with a cooler full of sweet meat, but with two tiny newborn wild goats, as black as the dark night, whom I followed faithfully up and down the ridges and studied as if they were my children. I saw the perfection of young goats—their grave assurance; their great liquid night eyes; and their delicate preference for certain twigs and leaves, a fresh mushroom, a tiny fluff ball of dry seed, the bitter and the sweet.

Looking Again

The other day

I saw the porpoises after a long time of not seeing them. We were camped by the harbor, fishing, and they were in the entrance to the harbor—splashing and leaping their midmorning dance. They are always a pleasure to see, something that takes the anger out of my eyes and reminds me that the world is glistening and simple for those with the grace to see it. And so, mulling over my constant anxiety about this or that, I look up for a moment to see a splash of white in a field of constant blue. I am alerted to think that it indeed might be the porpoises, returned for a while.

If the sea is calm, it's not hard to spot them, for you have only to consider the white water and try to figure out if it is caused by wind or current or rocks; if not by those, then it is likely to be something big and alive splashing in the water. A big tuna looks like a porpoise; and the wash from a boat looks like porps. I would often be deceived by the wash of a power-boat and fancy for hours that I was seeing all kinds of por-poises when I was looking only at my desire to see them, re-flected in the trail left by a passing boat. But now, after some years of looking and some thoughtfulness about what it is that I am looking at or for, I am not too often fooled by my desire.

Look for a splash of white water where there is no other, then look for the wind line or the current line or the passage of a boat. If there is no other white water visible and if the splashes come and go in the same area, then it is probably a school of porpoises. Why they are called a school is a mystery, for there is nothing in their life that in any way suggests school to me. In fact, I always thought of a school as fish of all about the same size, for they all seem to be birthed about the same time. A big school of *akule* or *ophelo* is fish of the same age and experience. But the porps aren't that way at all, and they certainly don't seem to have their babies all at once. I have never seen more than a few babies in a big group of porps at any given time, and I would guess that it's much more convenient and safe for the porps not to have too many babies at once, because of their vulnerability and the work of taking care of them.

So the school is out there fooling around in the morning, splashing and leaping, gliding in twos and threes with long fluttering and beating lines, hugging and chasing and playing and talking something to each other and to the sea. From the shore you can see the sun glisten on their dark backs or see the white-water spray as one or the other of them races from deep down to clear the surface and spin and twist in the air and fall full-out flat on the yielding water. Being a porpoise in the morning seems lovely and vigorous.

But the porps are not in school. There are no rows of seats or desks or long corridors, and there are no books and pens and video cassettes, but there may be, for all I know, a teacher or teachers. Animals often seem to learn from one another. At least, each mother is a teacher of essences.

Animals are often my teacher, more often than humans are, because humans mostly talk, whereas animals do. And what they do is often surprising. My dog is a teacher of essences. When I am dancing hula for myself, trying to work out the kinks and strains caused by too much thinking and being still, he will come into my dancing room and jump on me, ready to play. He wonders what it is in me that is so sluggish that doesn't respond, but just keeps up my slow silly twisting and bending, when I could be biting and jumping and really moving.

I am sure the porps would do the same if they could come into my dancing room, for my efforts at movement must seem like barely a start to them, who are always in constant motion.

The disease of this time must surely be a stiff neck, from the unrelieved effort of carrying around this heavy head, and propping it up so much of the time to look at something twenty-four inches or smaller. I notice now, after having spent some time in the water, where there is relief from the vertical and horizontal, that human life is lived on a flat plane. There is the flat bed and the flat seat and the flat floor, and many people cannot navigate the slightest unevenness of ground without losing their balance. So we have flat shoes and flat sheets and flat tables; and a jump of no more than three feet from rock to rock is formidable and challenging—almost impossible.

There are still old women around here, women raised on the ground rather than on the floor, who at seventy or so can sit hunkered, feet on the ground, knees bent, ass nearly touching the ground. They sit like graceful birds and fold their wrinkled brown hands around their folded legs, and being comfortable that way, sit for long times, with grace upon the earth. When I see women like that, my eyes fill with admiration and I know that I am seeing a teacher sitting.

Maybe that part of me which is reluctant to encourage you to go out and look at animals is my feeling that it is some kind of intrusion. What I need is to center my own animal consciousness, my own sensing, rather than enroll in the school of the porpoises. Yet doing that, we might know, then, a vastly different way.

Water. Water and the space of water and the color of water and the touch of water. The smell and taste of salt, the rush and glide of waves and currents, the caress of the sea.

Movement, a lifelong dance. A very lovely man I know, a scholar and a gentleman, is a student of porpoises and a teacher of humans. He sees the porpoises' movement as much like a football game, with a kind of coded game play, which he teaches his students to use when describing their movements. "Porpoise A at 7:06 turns sixty degrees north to northeast and proceeds for seventy yards toward . . ." This kind of description fills pages and pages of notebooks, and his students sit in the hot sun with binoculars and stop watches, charting the game.

My idea of describing porpoises might be to make a big-screen, color movie of surfers and hula dancers and porpoises, all superimposed on each other, creatures flowing through sparkling tunnels of silver blue foam. The sound track would be the sweet sound of humans singing of their love of moon and stars, water falling and falling over great cliffs into the shining sea, while young boys glide like seabirds on immense foaming, roaring waves. That is our correspondence, a sharing of grace and ability, a devotion to the sea and the life she gives so freely and with such abiding beauty.

I have not yet swum in the star dark sea and seen the shining path of the full moon rising from under the surface. I would imagine that it is as lovely as the day sun shining through the silver mirrored blue. We have been taught that night is a time of fear and danger, and this notion still holds me in its hands, so I have not yet gone into the night sea. But I have gone swimming in a pelting rain and watched the gray mist above turn into a sequined ceiling as the big drops spatter the surface and return to the sea.

There are many different ways to make sense, or story, out of one's experiences. School teaches us to select a reason, an answer, which is the right one, the only one. And given this disquieting and abiding "why" for a companion, we often torment or aggrandize ourselves with the answers to a lifelong succession of whys, as if the world we live in had not her own reasons, far too subtle and complex for human mentation ever to take hold of. But for the why-askers and the why-answerers there is reason and analysis to help this unwieldy process along, and the English language has embroidered itself into a vast catchbag of words heaped upon words, as if words were answers.

To be rock-bottom honest and plain, I can only say that I haven't the faintest idea of what whales or dolphins are doing except what my eyes see them doing, which is mostly moving around in the water, keeping company with one another, and making noises in the sea. I see mother whales with baby whales, and I see mother porpoises with baby porpoises, but I cannot for sure say that they are mothers, for I have never been able to say for certain what the sex of a whale is. I trust only the association, and it may be that the mother is really an uncle, babysitting for the afternoon, or an aunt or a father. The truth is that whales won't hold still for much studying, and neither will the porps. So even though I have seen porps and whales swimming along this coast at various times for five years or so, and I do recognize a few as ones I have seen before, I could no more draw you a diagram of their social relation-

103

ships than I could the relationships of the family of the man in the moon. And I have not the heart or the stomach for trying to track them with beepers and colored plastic streamers, or to eavesdrop on their intimacies with high-powered microphones and long lenses.

My bias against cameras and binoculars is simple enough. It is based on my own aversion to being looked at that way, of being invested with that distant quality of object. It is my abiding belief that the life we live and give is the immediate one, and not the one realized in some distant future. What we give to animals at the moment of giving is the fact of our relationship. If we give them respect and honest attention, that is how they know us, and that is the bridge we travel toward one another.

For these reasons I caution about looking at whales or dolphins or anyone, for that matter, as if there were no feeling there, no need for privacy or nicety, as if the looked-upon were indeed only objects for our restless and consuming curiosity.

I have seen people on a boat, centered in the glowing circle of blue sky, blue sea, and pastel islands for a few precious minutes of their lives, miss all that happened just next to them because the camera had to be wound or the lens wouldn't focus at the right time. So, instead of leaving with something seen fully with eyes open, they have only the frustration of the missed picture, which, if achieved, would only have given them a small gray speck on a tiny square of plastic and would never have given the rose-blown memory of whale breathing or the great crash as she plummets back into the sea. The picture would never give them her eye, looking squarely and cleanly into theirs, as creature gazed at creature, companions under the sun.

Traveling

Traveling by foot,

or at the pace of an animal, is far different from being carried, or sitting still while something moves you.

The world is much bigger when you travel on foot, with eyes open to the loveliness of green, the colors of the blue sea and sky, the velvet rainbow arching over the fields. Clearly you can see the rain misting over the hills, the sky opening and closing with the clouds, the wet earth colors changing in the changing light.

There is great luxury in being able to walk on this earth in the evening—the grass of the pasture is warm and inviting, the horses call to each other at sunset, the owl silently hovers over the field in the rose gray light, the tall pines look high over the island and sing in the wind.

In the morning I drink my coffee on the veranda and watch the cats lying in the shade of the *ti;* they turn green and yellow eyes here and there; stretch, leap, and preen; cluster on top of the wash-line pole. Seven cats watching the world go by, leaping at butterflies, sleeping in the sun, waking and stretching in the moonlight.

Animals are perpetually licking and cleaning themselves. The owl cleans her feathers in the dawn light; the cats scratch and lick; the horses nuzzle each other; even the flies clean their feet; and the winged ants preen, like cats, in candlelight.

Animals take care of their coats and feathers, and they

clean their feet carefully, picking out thorns and stones. Dolphins clean each other and lick each other's wounds. Dogs clean their cuts with their own tongues; and my dog cleans my cuts, too, thoughtfully and carefully.

Animals use their mouths, their tongues, cleaning and licking and nibbling. The horses listen to the sound of their own chewing and to each other's calling, to the sounds of cars and people, and watch the owl with sweet wings beating over the darkening grasses.

The owl paces herself with the moon's light; the fish float on the moon's currents; the plants follow light, sun and moon turning, opening and closing. The long green leaves with the red ruby ribs are a tangle of jewel leaves; and glowing among them are the glistening ripe tomatoes, adding to the intensity of a garden patch in the late afternoon's soft light, in the dappled shadows of the banana leaves. The immense imponderable beauty of nature and her treasures of light and color, forgotten by man.

There is no time when the dawn begins exactly. There is night and darkness, the stars shining brilliantly in the pulsing gray velvet dark, pinpoints of rainbow light that flash and glow. There is the time when it is colder and the sky is intense and bright, and then a slight quality of change: a bird calls, once; there is a rustle as a mouse goes; the gecko chirrups; the light shifts; the stars less bright. Then the slow opening of the dawn light and color as the deep brilliant night of stars shifts into the coming softness of morning, and the faint lightening of the sky over the house of the sun.

The air stirs; the wind calls softly. The gecko chirrups again, five calls, deep in the throat, clicking. The mynah stirs in his sleep, then resettles on the branch. The mouse goes over

108

the wall and into her house. The sea whispers her calm song as she foams gently over the rocks; the *vana* wave their spines. In the deeper pools the *ophi* suck the living stone; fish sleep in their caves or float motionless over the coral, drift and eddy and flash their iridescence in the tide's wash.

The goat sits in the dawn light chewing, her great star-gathering eyes open and silent, chewing, chewing, and listening to the sea surge over the fallen stones.

Many of us think we are trapped when, in fact, we are trapped only by habit or by our desire to somehow insure the future. Our lives become a perpetual seeking after a tomorrow that never arrives, a tomorrow when what we dream of will come to us, or a tomorrow when our nightmare will ride unharnessed. And lost, then, in a dream of a better—or worse —tomorrow, we attach ourselves to the immense labor of outwitting disaster or securing happiness. It is always later that we will finally take the chance, that we will loosen the buckles and trappings of security and sniff the dew-wet grass as a child would, or a colt, or the most insignificant mouse.

I watch us, people, do this, while I watch animals move so surely through the sights and sounds, scents and textures, of their houses. And it seems there is something unformed about people who seek the perpetual security of sameness, which dusts their eyes and dries their throats; it seems silly and fearful.

I remember canceling my health insurance when, with every bill, I received a letter trying to scare me into continuing my payments. The letters said if I didn't pay now, I wouldn't have it later—when I really needed it. That seems to be the thread that weaves life into a crazy quilt of anxiety and fear.

If there is a counterpoint here, it is the observed difference between the life of the smallest and most insignificant wild animal compared to the life of the most powerful man or woman. That comparison seems to leave me no doubt about the wisdom of nature and the confusion of human thought.

The boy who drowned three weeks ago flung himself into the sea in a moment of extreme elation, and for all I know is riding the sweet currents of air and flying with the long-tailed tropic bird. Meanwhile his parents mourn something they—and we—will never understand and never know.

Just as the word *birth* cannot describe the process, neither can the word *death*. And *blue* is a word that cannot possibly say anything of all the colors of the blue sky and the blue sea. All our words are much like signs propped in front of a living, mutable nature in a vain attempt to own a shifting reality.

Yesterday we went down to Keomuku to throw net and caught twenty or so exquisite pulsing gasping *manini*. Their small mouths quivered while their tails beat in the airy emptiness of the fish bag in an effort to hold on to life. Then they went flat and limp, eyes glazing over in the unfamiliar air. I looked at the small jewel fish dying in the bag and could only wish them peace, so that when I eat them, they do not stir guilt in my gullet and make me choke on their bones, actually or figuratively. That there is a transfer of form and life, that is given; that is immutable in this mutable world, and to accept that transfer with grace and understanding is my task. But I try not to be so absorbed with it that the issue of death becomes the only frame through which I see and love.

This business of eating what I see dying and of looking at the long face of the barracuda, teeth bared in the soup pot, is

110

a contact I maintain with life's actuality, and that contact keeps me free of the need to fantasize. The head of the barracuda staring out, a firm fast swimmer in the coral just hours before, now food for me and for my cats, is my immediate touch with life's given intensity and beauty. To the barracuda I give my thanks for sustaining me.

If the spirit of the boy is floating free in the updrafts of the salty cliffs while his parents mourn a wax-embalmed corpse in its coffin, then perhaps the barracuda and the *manini* swim free in me, and I am endowed with their grace.

I guess that what I am saying is that the riddle will always remain a riddle, and we have ways we can live with it, and the way of fear and insecurity is not the only way. I wish the boy's parents would cast off the black and go swimming in the sweet blue sea he flung his life into; that would be a more fitting tribute than the memory of the wax corpse.

When I lived inside an office and the only news I received of the world outside came in the form of pictures or print, it seemed indeed as if the whole earth were dying, and it was truly for me. I had taken myself away from what was renewing and alive and lovely. In that mournful state it was easy to imagine a vast symbology of life and death, so that a dying whale could stand for an entire planet. By some effort—not much, for imagination takes little real effort—the prevention of that death, as if death could be prevented, would save the earth.

Now I know better, for I know the earth is vastly stronger and more alive than any fantasy I might have of her, born between four walls and under a ceiling. I see that what keeps most people from giving themselves to the moment of loveliness is fear, fear of loss, of being hurt, of dying.

111

There is a difference between that all-purpose, exhausting fear of the unknown and the reality of the moment, which may have a particular danger attached and which may call for strength or wisdom or caution or luck. When my young horse rears herself up in front of me, I don't get silly and poetic and let her trample me, but I step aside and use my strength and thought to keep us safe, for, in fact, our safety and well being is mutual. I do not get silly and challenge gigantic waves with no more skill than my presumption, nor do I uniformly fear the blue water because there might be a shark swimming there. If there is a shark, then I use caution and am respectful.

There is something that is not categorical in reality, but is specific and actual; that is the something that is listened to and respected, and that is the unfolding of this life.

The story that nature tells is very, very slow, and she tells it softly, in a vast space of time changing as the light of each day and night unfolds and shifts. The rainbow is much like a day, present for the moment in all her colors, intensely glowing. It is the sequence from dawn to dusk that is given to us as a gift, for the moment.

There is the calendar that is a piece of paper with boxes on it; and there is the calendar that is a watch face printed with numbers in a circle; and there is the calendar of the day/night and of the sun riding the sky and of the moon following the sun —each circling its provinces. That time, of the day/night and of the sun/moon, is long and slow and stately and not broken by boxes and numbers, but is marked by the changing color of light, from and through all the shades of morning and midday and evening, and midnight and early dawn and sunset, and all between.

The time lived in this day/night is the calendar of animals and plants and is the calendar of the sea and of the wind and rain and the lives of mountains. All that lives follows this calendar as surely as there is breath on land and air filtering out of water in the gills of fish; and this rhythm, the rhythm of nature, pulses in us with our blood and comes in and out of us with each breath. There is no beginning and no end, just as there is no instant when black changes into gray or sunlight into darkness, for the time of nature flows like the sea and like the unfolding of seeds in the warm earth, and is and always will be a mystery.

I look at the smallest seed from the small blue flower of the coleus and nearsightedly think it is a mouse turd. I let my mind go rumpling about a mouse in the house and then look again to see it is a small seed from the drying flower; and that seed is just the beginning of the mystery that unfolds in the coleus. That mystery is so strong and sure that the torn branch can grow again and send out long silky roots in the sake vase, in the water that comes through pipes from the deep earth.

The branch cut from the tree lies with the other cut branches in the rubbish heap and sprouts flowers, and planted, years later, it sends down roots and grows. The *plumaria,* when cut, puts out white milk to cover her wounds, sticky white milk that is somewhat toxic to humans, but is the blood of the *plumaria* healing herself.

I do not plant tomatoes, but throw the overripe tomatoes from last year's plants on the ground, where they wait and become a vast tangle of tomato plants, growing through the veranda, overwhelming, succulent, the tomatoes hushed and dewy in the red ruby leaves of the swiss chard.

A seed is thrown on the ground and splits open and sends

113

out a filament of root and takes hold and becomes, year after year after year, a recurring tomato plant.

The dolphins are mysterious; they live in water and are not accessible except by great effort of will and machinery, and then only for a few moments out of the long slow beating time of their liquid days and nights in the sea. They are certainly more mysterious than the tomato plant, whose life is unknown to me, except in glimpses of the unfolding leaves or the small yellow flower that becomes a tomato—to be boiled with the *manini* with ginger root, garlic, and onion; to become soup or medicine or both.

How then to travel as a human in search of that essential grace the universe bestows upon herself so carelessly, and with such abandon. To travel lightfooted and strong, balanced, in harmony with the breathing of the earth, the whispering of the sea, the steady pulsing of tides and blood, and the particular songs of trees and streams. How to then cast off the trappings of future need and of fear and be elevated to essences, as an animal might go, fully conscious on this earth.

I go alone or in company, trying not to crowd out the sights and songs with inner chatter, not even trying to understand, for there is no such thing as understanding, but to let the colors of sunlight and moonlight flood freely through, as freely as the tides.

The human body, all parts usable and being used: self-cleaning; self-healing; eyes washed with salt; blood flowing strongly, pushed by the great heart that beats in each of us, nourishing brain and marrow. Moving, dancing, grimacing, tossing my head spiritedly as if I were the filly, as if I were the dolphin.

The Sea
as Physician

There she is, glistening, immense and vague before you, the mother of life on this earth as surely as the sun is the father, full of symbols and stories, the vast vessel of ocean glittering to the horizon, serene and beautiful, unknown.

We run ships on her surface, like tiny water beetles charting courses by stars and charts; we fly planes over her, the limitless blue glimpsed beneath the clouds, noticed briefly between the dry martinis and the flickering screen. We hunt her for treasures of rock and flesh. The biggest ships ever conceived are fly specks on the sea. We talk of typhoons and hurricanes and pretend that the gray pictures of swirling clouds have something to do with the imponderable power of wind and water.

And she is gentle, too, as a baby on a spring morning, lapping flicks of foam on silvered sand, calm and beckoning, as intimate as the human hand.

I believe her to be the essential doctor, the great healer, cleansing body and mind, restoring soul and circulation as the tides beat their constant rhythm on the shore, as sun and moon circle the sky and give us light and love in return for nothing except the appreciation of taking.

Nowadays believers in modern medicine ask to be healed with no effort or conscious awareness, as if the doctor were an all-purpose omnipotent god who needs only to glance at us in order to ascertain the mystery, as if he could produce out of his bag of tricks a tiny pill, of no taste or texture, that would miraculously heal us with no pain or quality, a nonthing designed to overcome all nature's processes.

Ancient medicine, folk medicine, recognized the need to restore harmony of body and mind and understood that harmony was health. Modern medicine is a response to our harried lives; it allows us to keep doing what we always do; it prescribes this or that chemical to overwhelm the body's crying need for rest and comfort and the mind's crying for beauty and love. But then ancient medicine came from nature and knew the close relationship between food and medicine and prayer and was not afraid to touch. Nowadays we do not commonly think that the touch of friends and relatives can heal or comfort.

The touch of the sea is healing and relaxing. The warm salt water washes away dirt and infection, bathes us in the same precious fluid that flows inside, relieves tired joints and bones from the continuous necessity of holding up our weight, gives us the freedom to fly.

I see a spa beside the sea—dolphins playing and spinning offshore; people relaxed on the sand, sleeping beneath the stars, listening only to the soft sounds of the surf murmuring or the calling of the wind in the palms. It is a place to rest and restore balance and wisdom, a place to come to bear babies and heal wounds, a place not to be beautiful in, but to look out at and see the beauty that is given.

The sea is doctor, and the earth provides us with medicine, and I would rather dig root and pick leaves to apply to a wound or ache than to go to the clinic and wait in that dreary room to receive my expensive and confusing prescription. For even if the taste of the root is bitter, we need to mix the bitter with the sweet.

Some years ago a man who lives here would travel often to the city to be treated for a pain in his belly, and the wear and tear on his body and pocket was great for he would take time off work, travel on an airplane, drive through exhaust-filled streets, go to a big hospital, and wait for a long time to be admitted into a harsh white room where he was once more examined for his terrible pain. After some years of this, he decided to try a simple old remedy and went instead to his garden and picked some leaves from a cactus plant. He soaked them in water in a glass jar and drank the bitter, clear juice of the plant. His pain diminished, and he continued the treatment. Now the pain is gone, and the plant still grows in his garden.

It is a common plant, the aloe; and it is succulent, with yellow juice, very sticky and cool. If you rub it on your burned or torn skin it will instantly comfort and heal. A wound inside is not much different from a wound outside, and what will heal and soothe a burn or a cut will also heal or soothe an ulcer, which is a fancy word for a cut that doesn't heal. The only difference is that you must be able to swallow the bitterness, which was, I guess, part of the ancient prescription. Whoever thought that medicine would be tasteless and featureless?

If you are to consult the ocean to help relieve your pain, you must be willing to get wet. And think of how, not too long ago, human beings were introduced to this earth.

Imagine then the sea as midwife. Instead of the harsh white light, the cold metal instruments, the strangers, the strangeness, think of bearing a new baby by the sea. Imagine the warm fire glowing and flickering, the clean mat spread on the clean earth, the sound of the surf soothing, stars shedding their soft fragrance, the distant deer calling their young on the mountain, the gecko chirruping, the sleeping birds as companions, the long cool quiet night waiting to welcome the new baby.

Lying there by the fire, warm and nourished by the night sky, by the warm steam coming off the sea, listen to the soft murmur of friends talking, of family singing and playing music, waiting with you to receive the baby. And you pushing, pulling, straining to bring out from inside, muscles working, contracting, laboring—to bring into warm arms the root out of the blue darkness, the child, the genealogy. The seed of man and woman, mixing, growing, taking form, waiting to come out into the sounds of the earth at night; the sea's quiet foaming on the dark stones, on the white glistening sand; the silky palms rustling like soft rain; the wind stirring, carrying coolness. Warm and nuzzling, the baby comes out, wet and breathing this sweet new air, crying, calling, stretching out —licking, holding and touching this new baby, you wash him in the sea, in the warm salt sea.

Swimming

It is morning; the sea is before me, vast and shining. She is mother, doctor, teacher, *kumu*. I am filled with the confusion of just waking; my mind is a chaos of faintly remem-bered dream and memory and imperfect sensing. My body is stiff and uncomfortable, weakened from too much sleep; my blood is sluggish, and my neck is sore. It is a common morning, filled with the softness of the earth's waking and filled with my general discomfort.

I go to Manele to swim. There is little surf; the water stretches clear and transparently blue green in the shallows, darker blue and glistening at the horizon. From my perch on the beach I can see the coral clearly under the water, marking a darker blue, a deeper yellow green. This small body of water, a tiny bay in the vast intricacy of coastline, is familiar and com-forting. I have seen its many moods, from big surf tumbling to gentle quiet lapping. For a space of a few hundred yards I can find my way from the bottom, know where the *mamo* cloud the water near the surface with their glowing yellow dazzle. I know where the *manini* is most likely to be found, and I am no stranger to the quiet resting of the big *weke* on the sand— dreamlike, they float there, hardly stirring the bottom, so com-fortable, so at home.

There is no one on the beach, and the sea glows and shimmers. The sand is unmarked except for the pattern of crab feet and one lone plover. The surface is calm. There is no wind, and the foam curls and glistens around my feet as I step into the sea. Holding mask and fins in my hand, I walk out to where the water is deep, beyond the shallow shelf of sand, and dive open-eyed into the salty water. The blurry haze of blue green, shifting light greets me and cleans my morning-tired eyes. I bend down and put on my fins underwater and surface, brushing away the hair from my eyes.

After the first tentative stretching and bending, I whisk myself around, wetting my hair and stretching my skin. Lying back and getting the hair out of my eyes and off my face, I settle my mask—adjust the strap and snorkel—and lie face down in the water, relaxed and ready to go. The sunlight shines on the sandy bottom, casting a diamond shadow of golden shifting light that looks much like the scales of a great fish. I think of the bottom of the shallow sea patterned with fish scales from the sun and swim above the golden light lines and head out to deeper water.

A lot of people put on their masks and fins on the beach and then awkwardly try to get into the water, unable to see clearly and unable to walk easily. This has always seemed silly to me, and I don't know why they do it that way, unless they have seen too many underwater movies. I have also seen a lot of people with masks and fins on walk backwards into the ocean, and this seems dangerous, for there is no way to judge the coming waves if you have your back to them. So I suggest that you learn the technique of putting on your gear when you are in the water, beyond the surf line; and, anyway, it is good to be able to take off your mask and snorkel and put them on in the water in case you need to adjust them while swimming.

Swimming in a calm sea with mask and fins is almost effortless, for the fins will help keep you afloat and give you plenty of moving power; the mask will keep the salt out of your eyes and allow you to see and breathe easily.

The waters that I swim in are safe if you watch the currents and do not attempt big seas or turbulent water. The sharks have lived here for a long long time and do not much bother. The rays are often awesomely big, but sweet-faced and gentle; the creatures that poke and sting do, but they are easy to avoid. The main danger is the human mind, which has great ability to create danger and panic out of its own imaginings. Still, I would not swim too far from shore alone, and I am often uneasy in murky water. When I am uneasy and uncomfortable, I swim close to shore or stay on the beach and wait for a more relaxed mind.

The very few times I have been in danger in the sea, I have found an inner voice to guide me, or the voice has found me through my confusion and fear.

There is a story that I read in a book that I like immensely. It is the story of a man, a local man, who found himself in the water after his small boat sank. He called out and asked if he had any 'aumakua (family gods) in these parts and implored them to come quickly for he was miles from shore and in rough and stormy seas. The fact that the story was retold testifies to the success of his petition.

A few years ago I went to Maui and in Lahaina rented a small kayak to pass a few hours. The man who rented me the kayak told me how to get through the reef into the deeper water and very carefully pointed out the channel because he could see I had no experience and ability. After paddling around inside the reef for a few minutes, I decided to go out; and, instead of heading for the channel, I thought I would just go through the surf line as I had seen others do so easily. Judging that the surf was low and the sea not rough, I thought it would be easy to just pass through a few incoming waves and be past the reef. As I got closer to the surf line, I saw that there were more waves coming in than it had seemed from a distance, but I went into them anyway.

I got through one or two waves, then they started to get bigger, and there were more and more coming in, so it became clear that I was going to dump the kayak and myself in the surf. I grabbed for my mask and fins and put on my mask, try-ing at the same time to hold the boat at an angle to the incom-ing surf, and went over and out. I dropped out of the kayak like a stupid stone and found myself swimming in the breaking waves. I headed out past the breakers and saw the man who had rented me the kayak paddling toward me.

He shouted at me to leave the kayak alone, and I let go, hoping the waves would carry it onto the beach. Floundering in the surf, trying to adjust my mask, I headed for shore, swim-ming through the breaking waves over the sharp coral and del-icately waving arms of the *vana,* afraid to be moving so fast and out of control, for the surf was breaking no more than two feet over the coral. Then, out of the confusion and fear, a voice spoke clearly inside my head. It was my own voice, but not my own; and it said very clearly, "Go with the waves, just go with the waves;" and I made myself as light as possible and let the waves carry me in over the reef. It was easy, so easy, once I stopped fighting the sea and, instead, let her carry me. I believe now that the voice always rests inside, ready when necessary

126

to guide me past my inexperience and confusion as long as I can control my panic enough to hear it speak. It is as if, coiled inside, it is an ancient wisdom, greater than my own, yet my own, that can guide me.

When I came here, I met someone who would often thank the place we were at for the goodness it had given us—the fish, the easy time, the good weather, the good luck. It was a simple thanks, said aloud without self-consciousness, just a thank you for the weekend, or a thank you for the fish; then we would go on our way, a little wet spot on the ground where we had poured some beer as our aloha. I found in that form, in that relationship with landscape and with luck, some-thing immensely appealing. It was easy to practice; it was given as the recognition of having once more been blessed. So now when I enter the sea, spoken in my heart is the wish for the blessing of the sea to be on me and on those I love.

It's sometimes hard to ask for this blessing when the beach is crowded and everyone is watching everyone as if there were some kind of contest involved in which no one, no matter how strong or beautiful, could ever be good enough to win. I see that contest enacted over and over and see the effect it has on people. And it is sad when it applies to nature's sweet gifts of sun and sea for it turns the beach into a backdrop for a play of uneasiness, instead of a comfortable place to put ass on ground and hand in sand and body in water. I know women who won't go swimming, and they know how, because they are ashamed of the way their bodies look in a bathing suit—as if the fish cared how we dress. Sometimes people will travel thousands of miles to reach this shining transparent sea and sand, and they'll be afraid of getting their hair wet or sand on their feet; and so they'll sit, staring at the sea, lost in a dream of themselves being there and never taste the salt or stretch their muscles in the comfort of the foaming surf.

This fear or distaste of nature, as if she were dirty, as if she were diseased, denies us the immense abiding comfort of warm earth and sand, of salt washing away the caked dirt of lotions and potions and the grime of civilized life.

Swimming, too, sometimes becomes a kind of contest, a kind of dogged determination to reach from here to there, as if there were a here or there in the sea.

Once I came up on the surface not more than an arm's length from a big booby bird, who stared at me, as astonished as I; then, saying something, he took flight. I remember his yellow beak and the surprised look in his eyes as my head popped out of the water.

Now again is the time of the rays' mating, and a family of them came in close to shore, really close; and as we watched from the rocks, we could see their brown gleaming backs, dotted with white, fluttering around each other. The big one was in front, and the other very close, and the small ones behind, fluttering in white water as if they were flying.

In the water the rays turn their porpoise-faces to me—long noses, beautifully tapered foreheads, and the same kind of a smile. They float past, long tails streaming, their butterfly flesh wings, immense and sure, slowly bearing them past.

And the *kala*, so seductive, wagging her streaming filaments of blue violet light over the coral head, keeping her place there, slowly waving her elegant tail, looking around, long filaments of *kala* flesh elaborately flowing after her.

The squid pulses his changing colors over the coral, drapes

himself over each rock, digs holes in the sea, and waits there with eye looking out, or swims a mantle, a pulsing membrane, transparent and serene, coursing for the bottom and reaching, flowing over the coral, changing color again. Brown and speckled brown and deep velvet brown and pale sand colors pulse through the squid's skin as he flows along the coral.

Now there is squid in my stomach and in the cooler. Life then is given and goes; it is not a tragedy; it is something changed and transmuted, and perhaps the very first stuff of the universe is in me now, for nothing really goes away for where does it have to go. It must still be here, in me, in you, in dolphin, in squid and *vana*, changing form, casting rainbow bubbles, pushing through damp earth to flower and fruit and dry and wither and flower again. I am often surprised at the appearance of a plant, growing out of the soft ground, that I never planted, but was there, waiting, long before I looked at that patch of moist earth I now call my garden.

In the early morning I go to the tide pools with my young friend, and we sit flat-assed on the warm wet lava, the stones poking me. We look into the small worlds of hermit crabs, baby shells, *gouby* fish, and whoever else lives there. The hermit crabs have tiny twinkling black and white feet and pale blue eyes and live in shells perfectly matched to the color of their speckled sand-filled holes. When they travel, they look like tiny clumps of sand moving over the tide-wet rock; then, reaching a sand-filled *puka*, disappear and come out again and walk around on the dark rock. And others, living in the smallest perfection of dark, twisted shell, are equally at home on the black lava—hermit crabs, miniature duplications of their homes, walking around in the morning on twinkling feet.

And my small friend says, "Look at him, isn't he cute." She picks up the shell and crab, turning it over in her hand, so that the tiny claw comes out, and soon the whole crab appears, his blue eyes popping out and around, his perfect spider feet banded black and white, ready to get going.

The *goubys* look like fairy-tale fish with their flat dragon heads and big feathery feet fins. They pop from pool to pool, flutter over the dark rocks, hide in the *pukas* and jump again and again; they saunter in the early morning tide pool, looking for food, chasing each other.

The water in the shallow pools is warm, and we sit, faces peering at the water inches away, saying hello to hermit crabs and *goubys*. We watch them through the transparent film, looking up at the big waves booming in and foaming over the rocks. The surf is up, and the white water rushes in and out of the pond. The water is crystal clear and clearer, so that each drop from my dripping hair disturbs for a moment my view of the silver fish that cluster around my hand, nibbling and poking, brave and wary. I can see the absolute perfection of their markings—the tops of their heads outlined in dove gray and pale green and violet bands of light, their gold-rimmed eyes more iridescent than any earth-born gold, outlining a flat disk that at first looks black, but in some light is the color of lapis. The jewel eye of the *'ahole'* hole looks at me through the transparent water on the ledge of the pond, and my young friend, squatting over another pool, tells me of the marvels she is witnessing.

The *'ahole'* hole are curious, and we stare at each other through the surface with as much clarity as my vision has ever allowed, and I think about focal length and that maybe my glasses are to save me the effort of bending my head closer to what I might want to see; another cause for my stiff neck, never much having to bend it to look around.

Yet if I put my face very close to the water, I can see perfectly the hundred or so baby fish, each half the size of my hand; they turn their young eyes on this strange animal and look me over. And I see the flash of glowing silver as one turns sideward and reflects sunlight off of pure silver scales.

Animals and fish are exquisitely lovely. One day I summoned the courage to handle the dry body of the brown spider lying on my desk; I saw there, almost faded, the delicate beige lines of her markings, and the tiny withered dry mouth that once seemed so formidable in my dreams. My first visions of spiders came from comics, rather than from the brown-striped face of the spider. And I find that the feel of the dead spider in my hand is not much different from a feather; only the idea, the thought of the feel is so disconcerting.

The waves build up outside the point; from where I stand in the pond, I can see them curling and foaming, walling up out there, rolling in and cresting and foaming—the south swell, the weather is changing.

I can feel the difference in the water; the water is the same, but not the same; and even though it is as warm as summer water, it is not. It is this subtle change that tells me that summer is over and winter is coming. The whole sky is changing—the clouds banking up and gathering rain, the wind shifting—and then rain falls heavily on the dry side, so you can see and feel the sky turning around, the coolness coming. In the harbor the baby *akule* are swarming under the baited poles. The immense mass of young fish are waiting in the muddy water for their time to go to sea.

131

Sanctuary

Once, long ago, in an effort to celebrate nature inside a big cathedral, we made a tape recording of wolves howling and men singing Gregorian chant. We hung the big speakers high above the altar, facing each other over a great distance, and let the men and the wolves sing to each other in the big echoing space below. Inside, it worked pretty well, and something of the grandeur of man and animal sang there in the candlelit darkness.

I think the old meaning of the word *sanctuary* was that something sacred existed there and could not be denied by man or woman.

I dig for the root meanings of words, just as I might dig for the sweet potatoes in the sandy hills, looking for essences, looking for nourishment.

If I were to invent sanctuary, it would be just as I have found it, a place where we meet to give our most sacred to each other.

If I compare the sound of a man singing of his love of mountains and flowers with the sound of this electric typewriter, I would prefer to hear the man singing, just as I would prefer to have my body moving elegantly and gracefully in a dance given to the beauty of movement and the pictures my hands could tell in air.

I have no idea what the dance of the dolphins is to them, but to me, watching, it is lovely beyond description, languid and pulsing, the articulation of legs into tail that, I am told, is the history of dolphin. To move in water, to swim in warm water, seeing the light dazzle and the soft rays floating and slowly turning in the dappled shallows is sanctuary, that is, sacred. As is the sun rising over the mountain, lighting the dewy webs of spiders, outlining the waiting leaves and brushing the meadow with fog and mist, with the faint touch of water in air, water floating. The sea is the only place I know wherein I can fly easily, and turn and stretch and make bubbles of silvered rainbows and see the silver fly before me.

And whale swims in a sea actual and is very fast and can rise out of the water into air, a great plummeting diver in the sky, and fall with a booming echo that lights the sides of volcanoes with her sound. Whale is as she is and as he is.

I camped by the stone wall one night by myself. I came down from the town to get into the darkness and silence and thought that if I slept out by myself under the stars, I would relax and have the luxury of the beach unmarred in the early morning. I drove down and laid out my sleeping stuff in the back of the pickup and built a small fire to cook a piece of meat and cheer myself. The night soon exerted its peculiar magic, and I was happily drifting in it when I saw a flicker by the stone wall, just a small, dark shadow passing. I watched closely, trying to see between the shadows of the firelight on the

136

stones and the other shadow that had just passed. I sat still, listening and watching. Soon I saw a small mouse, the soft gray kind that darts here and there in the intricacies of mouse life. This mouse came foraging out of her hole in the wall, looking for whatever might be within reach. She was good company in the night, and I was relaxed and comfortable watching her go here and there in search of mouse happiness. Then I noticed that she was lapping at the mouth of a fallen beer bottle, that she was drinking beer. I watched as she went more and more into the bottle, until she was completely inside, drinking at the pool of beer left in the bottom, much like a cave explorer might drink at an underground stream. I watched her for a long time, and she never came out, and it was hard to tell if she was okay in there. I thought maybe she had gotten drunk, so I decided to find out. I gently picked up the beer bottle. It must have felt to her as if the proverbial sky were falling, like a great and fearful cataclysm, for she backed out of the bottle faster than a mouse can go and disappeared into the wall.

I felt an immeasurable happiness, as if, indeed, we, the mouse and I, were in the center of a charmed circle of fire, stars, and the sea's gentle lapping. I felt, then, and still do, as if that glimpse of a mouse was one of the highlights of my life, a funny flicker from another kind of living. Yet it was pretty simple—a mouse drinking beer by the fire.

It is these subtleties that are woven to form a natural tapestry of the quietest kind, a loom of soft memories of crea- tures and their adventures—the shine of a small eye in the darkness, the dedication of a spider laying eggs, the repetitive clicking of the gecko—which reassure me that the night world is in order: the barking of the deer on the mountain or the print of small feet in the sand that tells me someone passed not too long ago.

It seems in most books about nature there is a lot of action, a lot of events. Animals are stalking and killing and eating each other, and the weaving color is blood red. And the same goes with movies. We think we need a story told, and the only story anyone has been able to devise that holds interest is the story of life and death, with the events of life made exciting by death. The fish chase each other—chase each other around —and, I guess, hold onto their place, but the chasing seems as much like a game as anything else. The same *gouby* will come sneaking over to the same pool a hundred times a day, only to be chased away by the same other *gouby*. Certainly, at one time or another, they are hurt and do not recover, but that seems remote when you are watching them in the pond chase each other and glean goodies from the rocks. The abiding of *goubys* seems to be that they dart and flop and run into holes and eat and chase each other.

This morning the sun rose over the water through a veil of light rays, lavender and peach color. Maybe the great events in nature are the colors the sky takes at dawn and sunset and the particular beauty of the full moon rising, or the soul-stirring hopefulness in the new moon, a silver light in the pale sky of sunset.

For a while I had the luxury of living on a cliff, and I found a great affluence in being able to live in the cycle of moon and sun. My serene and comfortable moments came while I was lying under the sky, open to the earth and sea around me, watching the slow change from day to night come over the world as the colors slowly faded into darkness and the irre- placeable beauty of the star-filled sky settled over me. I heard all of the small sounds of the night—the deer calling, the geckos clicking, the birds briefly waking and then settling. There was no boundary between us, and I and the animals shared, equally, the same world. And in watching all that and living in and through that rhythm I saw how simple it was, how uncomplicated. Yet all of my training in thought was to complicate, to explain, to describe in order to achieve events—to make the world exciting. But it seems underneath all that human-created complexity is something simple and calm and stately: the earth and sea rolling in their time, changing and yet eternally the same. That is my best and most honest observation.

Although I cannot say that I saw enough of whales and porps to offer anything more than a glimpse, what I did see, and still see, seems to confirm that simplicity. They swim, they feed, they bear babies and caress each other, and fill their days and nights with what looks like love and play. If they think great thoughts, which was once an idea with much appeal for me, they keep it well hidden. I know now that thought is a minor and flaccid thing compared with grace of movement or with love given and received.

One night while I was sleeping on the cliff I heard a whale pounding her tail on the water just below. The sound was an explosion, a deep boom and then an echo, but of a quality far different from a man-made explosion. It was an immense reverberating, natural sound, waking in me a feeling of great joy at being able to sleep there under the sky with the sound of the waves circling the shore and the whale pounding and pounding her tail. Even in the dark I could see the white water flying as she crashed, again and again and again, on the surface of the placid sea.

In the morning there was, at her side, a subtle flicker of pale turquoise light, the water awash over the white belly of her new baby. I knew, then, that the sound I had been listening to all the night long was the sound of a whale giving birth.

Since then I have seen and heard whales pounding their tails on the surface, and it has not always been that they were giving birth. It seems, too, that they do it to make noise or maybe when they are angry, but I know also that the sound of the sea booming is the sound of an immense labor—a whale baby being born.

I think that if you take your time to go out and look at nature's events, they will come to you, as they do to me, in a rhythm and with a meaning all their own. I have never had much of a theory to elaborate, so without a theory to impose, nothing too orderly comes out, just a random collection of bits and pieces—fragments strung on memory, popping from pool to pool of thought, much like *goubys* pop from pond to pond.

Now it is October, the transition from summer to winter, a soft and comfortable month, when the sun is easy and the sea calm. Somewhere, far north of here, the whales are ready to swim the long passage, last year's babies strong and able; this year's mothers heavy; the young ones frisky; the old ones tired. Not too different from the people who will come to look at them for a moment of difference out of their lives.

This is also the time when the young of the *akule*, the *halalu*, are swarming in the harbor and the people are busy with baited bamboo or the new fiberglass poles, trying to catch fish all the hot long day. They salt and dry them and eat them raw with chili pepper and onions. It's hard to tell how many fish are in this small place, but there must be thousands, for every day hundreds and hundreds are caught, and the fishing might go on for three months or more before the *halalu,* for some reason of their own, will one day swim out of the harbor.

I saw a school of *halalu* once, swimming in the bay. I came upon it unexpectedly and thought at first I was seeing a coral head in the deep water. From a distance, I could see a misty shape reaching almost to the surface—a pyramid of flashing light. Then going closer, I realized it wasn't a coral head but a tightly packed ball of fish, slowly revolving in the same direction, the ones at the top spinning off and around and rejoining the mass. Ten thousand fish packed in that small space, serenely revolving clockwise over the sandy bottom in the deep water, silver sides flashing, gold eyes gleaming. With them was a big barracuda, three feet or more, hovering over the ball like a guardian, hardly disturbing the school. I didn't get too near, for I didn't want to spook and disperse them; so I hovered maybe ten feet away, watching them. Then from behind, as fast as light itself, the barracuda charged the pile and opened a great tunnel in the ball, carving out of speed and fear his own cavern of nothingness, and disappeared on the other side. I have no idea whether he caught on that charge; it seems impossible that he didn't. A school of fish is an efficient way of not getting caught, for it's hard to concentrate on one fish with a thousand, all the same, swimming around; and if you don't concentrate on one, you will get nothing for the rest will confuse you into failure. However, later it became clear that he did catch enough that day because for several weeks I would swim out to find the school and the barracuda together. Nothing after that equaled my first sense of awe at seeing the coral head resolve itself into a flashing silver pyramid of life.

The mynahs are fighting under the *keawe* in the early morning; I hear a great babble of scolding and see a blur of

141

white and black wings. It must be about food, but it could be about love or place. The argument is heated and noisy, but after the flourishing of voice and the fluttering and flying at each other, they all fly away and settle companionably in the tree as if nothing had just happened. There is no wounded or dead bird on the ground; it was just a good-natured early-morning squabble. Sometimes it seems when they fight like that, death can be the only result of such passion; yet they fly away together, no one perceptibly the worse.

The sounds of morning are the mockingbirds in their litany, the distant sweet cooing of hundreds of doves, the sharper voices of the mynahs, a plane overhead, people's voices laughing. Birds and shrimp join voices in this early-morning chant; the noise of the plane recedes. The loudest voice, the typewriter, is trying to send from here now, to there then, the sounds of this morning. The boat sways gently, and sunlight patterns and drifts across the varnished wood, and the mountain, dusty gray gold hot, shifts in the window of the companionway.

I once saw a whale blow an immense bubble under a boat, and a dolphin once pulled me to shore with his third arm, in answer to my unspoken fear.

Mostly I see people and the sea, the sun and the moon not metaphor, the mountain as a way to travel. I know that I give too much time to thinking and that my body grows stiff and unused from the effort of words and the lack of movement. It is good to walk barefoot on the rocks and take salt, carefully, from the little pools on the ledges. It's lovely to see the dol-phins and swim out to them, quietly, hopefully, comfortably.

I am not sure about advice; I have always been my own teacher; and the mountain, too, the sea, and friends are my

142

teachers. My dog teaches me, my horse teaches me, the ants drinking around a drop of fallen honey teach me. Sometimes people say something that helps the understanding, but mostly it's in color, in the smell of something—musky or sweet—the touch, the motion of life that teaches. *Kumu* in this language literally means "trunk"—the trunk of the tree, the source of nourishment. A *kumu* can be someone who knows a dance or a song, a way to build a fire, a way to listen. The old ladies who hunker on the grass are *kumu,* as are the glances of children and the way the owl rises noiselessly from the darkening grass and flutters over the meadow.

The porpoises are in school; they are twirling and flying over the sea and crashing back into the water. In the long hour of twilight, the *halalu,* running from the big fish, ruffle the lavender silk of the surface, sounding like pebbles thrown on the sea, silver bodies jumping clear as the big fish charges. Over and over, in the soft velvet twilight, the sun slowly going over the hill, the water and air growing darker and darker, the big fish chases the school. The sound scatters the silence, the boiling and fluttering of the water speaks of life.

The people have nearly all gone; a few remain in the ebbing night to watch the fish and listen to the sounds of the mountain. The mynahs cluster and chatter; the waves sing their shoreline song; dark shapes of the *keawe* stand outlined in the red light of the setting sun. The fish go toward the open water, slowly, darker blue against the darkening sea. It is part of another day and part of another night we are in, watching this slow weaving of fish and bird and mountain coming to rest.

Yesterday the porpoises were playing outside in the morning, pink-bellied babies breaking the surface in perfect unison;

143

already rolling, porpoising, in the glistening sea; and in the transparent green water, turning to look at us with great open eye, sleek and close, companionable.

My dog barks at them from the bow. It is the first time he has seen porpoises, and he is happy and excited and noisy.

This morning the sun rose in a cloudless sky after a warm still cloudless night of coming quarter moon, with Orion slowly turning overhead.

I look for the porpoises the same place I saw them yesterday. They are not there. The sea shines sequined light, dances and glitters. In the distance two volcanoes sleep in the sea, pale and misty, the high sky swirling ice crystals above them. People are fishing; mynahs flutter from the trees. It is time to go swimming.